BLING

bling

A STORY ABOUT DITCHING
THE STRUGGLE AND
LIVING IN FLOW

ANDY SETH

BLING

A Story About Ditching the Struggle and Living in Flow

ISBN 978-1-5445-0553-4 *Hardcover*

978-1-5445-0552-7 *Paperback*

978-1-5445-0551-0 *Ebook*

This book is dedicated

To all the homies in the struggle.

It's all good, baby baby.

CONTENTS

DITCH THE STRUGGLE

PREFACE

I wrote this book in five days. Yes, rounds of edits were part of the process, so the total time was longer, but the actual story flowed through me in just five days from start to finish.

The truth is, I never set out to write *Bling*. In fact, I had another book ready to roll when the message for this story came to me in a meditation. I meditate for an hour and a half every day, so I wasn't surprised when this message came to me out of nowhere. That kind of creative inspiration is a direct result of practicing what I teach in this book.

I didn't start writing the story immediately. A few weeks after that particular meditation, I was scheduled to deliver a speech to a program for emerging African American leaders in my community. I thought the message that came to me during my meditation, about a rapper going on his spiritual journey, was meant to be my keynote.

My wife Natasha suggested I head up to the conference site in the mountains a day early to turn the message into a speech. I got to my hotel, checked in, and ended up putzing around online, eating dinner, and hanging out in the jacuzzi. By 11:00 p.m., I had not written a single word. I laughed to myself thinking: *All right, universe. I showed up. I did my job. When are you planning on coming through here to help me deliver this?* I had zero stress about it, no anxiety, nothing. I was just open and ready.

When I sat down at 11:00 to finally start writing, the words poured through me. I was in a complete flow state. I tapped into the universe. From 11:00 p.m. to 2:45 a.m., I just wrote. I didn't read what I was writing, and I didn't edit it. I just wrote and wrote and wrote. *Bling* poured through me. By 2:45 a.m. I was at a natural stopping point. I laughed again, thinking: *Well, I have no idea what I'm going to do with this, because it's definitely not a speech.* I went to sleep surrendering, knowing that whatever was meant to be was meant to be.

I woke up the next morning and meditated. When I was sitting, the idea hit me: I needed to read what I wrote the night before, live, unedited, to my audience. I arrived at the conference and told the crowd, "Today I am going to read you something I wrote last night, and I haven't even read it myself. It's coming straight from the source, through me, to you."

For the next thirty minutes, I read what became the introduction and first chapter of *Bling*. When I finished, I got a standing ovation. It was amazing to see what followed. The Q&A lasted an hour and a half, an hour longer than scheduled. What was fascinating to me was that the questions were not about me. Typically, when I give a speech, it's a story about me and the questions are about my experiences. In this case, it felt like we were all on this journey together.

The questions people asked were all about the lessons from the speech and the journey that this fictional rapper I had conjured was experiencing. People related to the story and opened up about some of the pain and suffering that they felt. Some of them shed tears because they were being raw and real.

When I returned home, I told Natasha what had happened. We knew there was something more to this message and that it was definitely a story, not a speech. Natasha, out of the love and kindness of her heart, suggested once again that I go and write in solitude, this time for four days. I reached out to my friend Anil (the inspiration behind the character AI in *Bling*), who owns a mountain house that resembles a sanctuary, and asked if I could work solo from there. He didn't blink. I went up on a Saturday night, set up my environment and senses to trigger flow state, and started writing on Sunday morning. By Wednesday, my story was complete.

Writing a book can take people months, years—sometimes a lifetime goes by without them having ever done it. I did it in five days because I stayed concentrated in flow state, morning till night. I went into deep, hour-and-a-half meditations before writing, had no distractions or notifications, was surrounded by beauty and nature, turned off all other electronics but my laptop, and triggered all five senses to get into flow. Combined with my storytelling and writing skills, everything in the story quickly fell together.

Bling is a parable, a largely fictional story about a rapper named A-Luv who created one of the best-known albums in all of hip-hop's history. As his success grew, so did his collection of bling, cars, and houses. All the while, his personal life was falling apart. The minute he achieved something, he had already moved on to asking, "Now what?"

The "now what" question is the root of this story and is relatable to anyone who has done what they set out to accomplish and dreams of doing more.

This is not a how-to book. Instead, through storytelling, *Bling* reveals a five-step process to do the work internally that results in true inner peace while being totally creative and ambitious. You don't have to choose between Forbes and robes. I want you to know that you can have both. You don't have to struggle for your ambition, and you don't have to renounce the material world. You don't have to sacrifice time with your family, health, or happiness to achieve your dreams. You can be driven and good with what you have. You can be totally chill and chase greatness.

My own story influenced the main character and although I'm not a rapper, I was a professional DJ for almost a decade and went by the name of DJ A-Luv. I've never produced a track in my life, but I could hear the music inside me when writing this book, so I accepted this as a gift and decided to produce a soundtrack for *Bling*.

As far as I can tell, this is the first book to ever have an original soundtrack.

I grew up in a motel in LA until I was fourteen. We didn't own the motel; we just lived there. My dad collected the rent and my mom cleaned the rooms, communal bathrooms, and did all the tenants' laundry while she worked full time as a phlebotomist. When I was nine and my younger sister was three, our family declared bankruptcy due to my dad's failed business venture. He took a risk that didn't pan out. The bankruptcy crushed our family financially and it crushed my parents internally. When people talk about failing fast, I often wonder why they would talk about failing at all. I never had a safety net to catch me if I failed, so I desired safety and security, but I was also highly driven and ambitious to realize my life's potential.

My parents are typical Indian immigrants who stressed the importance of getting an education, and I was fortunate that they let me run free to hustle on the street. I never touched drugs or banged, but I was crafty and found ways to make money so I could have some fun.

I was academically strong and ended up earning full-ride scholarships to Culver Military Academy (high school) and Boston College. Education itself isn't entirely what changed my life; it was gaining access to a world that I never knew existed.

We didn't have the convenience of YouTube and the internet, but we did have libraries filled with books, and I read as much as possible in the self-help and business sections. I applied the lessons from these books to grow personally and to create a real business. I started my first company when I was thirteen and grew that into headlining as a DJ and promoting nightclubs till I was twenty-two.

Along the way, I started and sold two internet companies during college. By the time I graduated, I had three businesses under my belt.

Since then, I've been blessed with numerous successful businesses, and I've helped send hundreds of low-income kids to college on scholarship through my nonprofit work. I eventually reached a point where status, money, and ice didn't fulfill me. Civic leadership didn't totally fulfill me either. I felt like I had more to do and more to give, but I had reached the top of my frame. I have already lived a life that beat the odds, so I needed a new frame, and I knew the place to look was within me. No one else was going to tell me what the frame should be and even if they did, I wasn't going to listen. I wanted to live my own life, free of labels, and I needed to answer the most fundamental question: what do I want?

That's when I went through my own spiritual transformation. I came to realize that even though I had achieved a level of success that most people would give me props for, I still felt I hadn't lived up to my own potential. After I sold my last business, I had lots of time and resources, but not the answers.

My journey took me back to Laxman Jhula, Rishikesh, India, where my uncle, a jeweler, helped guide me on my spiritual path. I spent mornings till evenings in a highly concentrated state, asking him questions to help me connect the dots between the inner and outer worlds. He taught me lessons that his teacher taught him and that have been passed down for generations to only those who sought the truth. All my life I knew my uncle as a highly successful businessman and someone full of life and joy, but it wasn't until I started asking questions that the wisdom channeled through him to me.

My calling is to channel this Eastern wisdom to you in the Western world, in a modern way.

While the lessons in *Bling* have been taught for over 1,500 years by spiritual leaders and gurus, I always felt like they were too soft, and their words never hit me right. Don't get me wrong, these leaders and gurus provide great messages for people who get down with them; they just aren't my people. I figured if they weren't vibing with me, there must be other people, like you, who would love to learn the teachings in a fresh and relevant way.

Bling is a modern-day approach to spirituality inspired by the hip-hop culture. Hip-hop is a culture that is born out of the struggle and celebrates those who beat the odds. Its culture not only transformed everyone within it, it transformed society. Hip-hop has inspired my life and continues to be the biggest cultural force worldwide. Today there's a consciousness movement happening in hip-hop where leaders and artists are elevating their vibe and creating a shift to improve themselves and the lives of others. They are becoming more aware that there's more to life than being rich, and because they are cultural leaders, they can spread their message in a way that shifts society.

My goal is to help you find that inner peace while unleashing the creativity and ambition inside you.

We all know what it's like to feel like we aren't living up to our potential, like we should be more than we are. And that's the thing, it's a feeling. You can't achieve the feeling of self-realization through external things like money or status. Traditional spirituality has made the process of self-realization fluffy and in ways impossible to reach. But if you have a desire to understand yourself on a deeper level, without the foo-foo talk, then *Bling* will resonate with you.

The mental health tools help you ditch the struggle and live a life in flow where you feel entirely at peace and hyper-present, to the point where you actually sense the enormity of every moment in your life. The key to realizing your potential is meditation. I know tons of people have tried and failed at meditation, including myself. If you've struggled to make meditation stick because you couldn't sit still and clear your thoughts, then *Bling* is for you.

The entrepreneurial skills help you tap into an energy source that unlocks new levels of creativity and innovation within yourself. Great entrepreneurs aren't just innovative, they focus on the right things with an intense amount of concentration. Knowing the right thing to focus on is easy when you're deeply in tune with yourself, and when you have developed the skill to concentrate, you'll find your output is much higher quality and takes a fraction of the time that it takes others. This is how you hustle without burning out.

The behavioral psychology helps you understand the difference between what you *should* do and what you *will* do. This is known in economics as the behavior gap and as a behavioral economist who taught mindset tricks to the wealthy, I know how important it is to deal with what's real, not theory. Fifteen hundred years ago, there was a lot less distraction, and it's time the methods and teachings were updated.

The energy management techniques help you prevent burnout. When you are adapting your natural self to the rest of the world, you feel drained and exhausted. Burnout is avoidable and it all comes down to energy management. Keep your energy tank full and you'll succeed at life; keep it low and you'll always feel like you're behind. *Bling* explains how to manage, move, and direct your energy during meditation so you can retain more energy for the things that will help you realize your potential.

The life lessons help you avoid feeling lost, disconnected, or unrealized—that you never hit it big, never felt true love, or never became the person you always thought you could be. When you are in a state of anxiety, it's impossible to be in love with your life. Stress and happiness cannot coexist; you cannot be both at once.

The time-saving tools help you experience life at exactly the speed of time. If you find yourself saying, "time is flying by" or "man, that year went by fast," then you are experiencing time passing you by. Society accepts these expressions too quickly, and they're all indicators that you are not living in a concentrated state of awareness known as presence. When you're not fully present, you'll never experience complete love and gratitude for the moment.

I'm stoked for you to read *Bling* and go on a journey to master your mental health, build entrepreneurial skills, awaken your soul, manage your energy, practice meditation, and live life on a whole other level. Sending positive vibes your way as you read *Bling* and listen to the soundtrack.

Andy Seth
Denver, Colorado

ON A
MISSION

1

ON A MISSION

A-Luv stood on the balcony of his ten-million-dollar Malibu mansion, watching the waves crash on the sand in front of him. He held a vape pen in his right hand when the phone in his left hand began to buzz.

It was Rohan, A-Luv's agent, calling.

They had been planning A-Luv's first world tour, and A-Luv wanted his last concert to be in India. He asked Rohan to make it happen, and this was the day Rohan delivered the news.

"Yo A! Good news, playa. You're booked in Bombay!"

"*Dope!*" shouted A-Luv. "I knew you could do it, my man. Thank you!"

Rohan was happy to hear the excitement in A-Luv's voice too. They went way back and for years, Rohan watched A-Luv's fortune and fame skyrocket while A-Luv struggled with loneliness, self-worth, drug addiction, and failed relationships.

He lost some of his best friends in the game too soon, and people all over the world missed them: Prince, Michael Jackson, Tupac, Biggie, Heavy D, Big Pun, J Dilla, Phife Dawg, Mac Miller, and Nipsey Hussle. He could see his own life heading down any one of those paths. The relationships that didn't work out, the friends he lost, the family he stopped communicating with, his addiction to drugs, poor eating habits, and the loneliness and depression that often overtook his every waking feeling.

As much as Rohan tried to get him help, A-Luv resisted help from experts because he felt like they were either trying to change him, drug him, or both, and he didn't want to lose the creative edge that fueled his music.

"While you're in India, I arranged for you to visit my uncle Guddu in the Himalayas. He's a jeweler and I told him to hook you up!"

A-Luv loved his bling and was known for wearing gold chains around his neck, an iced-out Rolex, massive diamonds in his ears, and countless rings and bracelets. He was excited to check out that world-famous Indian gold and come back with some OG pieces. Growing up, he never experienced material wealth and now, he was all about it.

It had been three months since he got the call from Rohan, and the world tour was complete. The last show in Bombay sold out within hours when tickets went on sale, and the concert was epic. As he walked off stage for the last time on this tour, he could feel the crowd's energy and a sense of calm came over him. This is what he lived for—to move crowds and inspire them with his music.

But when the hype died down, so did the buzz, and feelings of emptiness quickly arose. He now sat on a plane leaving Bombay heading to a northern Indian town called Laxman Jhula, Rishikesh, to meet with Rohan's uncle, Guddu. He felt physically and mentally exhausted but the thought of scoring some new bling gave him just enough energy to make the trip. He loved the whole process of going into a showroom and being escorted to the highly secure VIP section, where champagne was being poured while white-gloved jewelers handed custom pieces to him one-by-one. He loved admiring how each piece looked on him and thinking of what people would say when they saw his new pieces. And more than anything, he loved how each piece was a constant reminder of how far he had come. From ashy to classy.

HIGH VIBE
LIFESTYLE

A-Luv grew up the son of Indian immigrants in a motel in LA, and from early on he cultivated his ability to write and rhyme. His storytelling ability was unlike anyone who had come before him—raw and real—and he had a gift for bringing listeners into his world with his songs. He hit the underground scene when he was fifteen, and by the time he was eighteen, he was working on his debut album. Top producers from LA were collaborating with him. They all knew he was a prodigy.

When the debut album dropped, it was an instant classic. For the second time in history, *Source Magazine* gave a debut album a 5-mic rating. Twenty-two years later, it's still known as a landmark album in hip-hop and widely regarded as one of the greatest, most influential albums of all time.

Every album he dropped after outsold the one before, his fame soared, and money filled his bank accounts. You could see it on him wherever he went—always blinged out. He had all the things: money, power, and fame. And yet, deep inside, he felt like none of his albums truly lived up to his first one. His fans knew it. The critics knew it. And worst of all, he knew it.

As the years went on, he found himself getting heavier into drugs and alcohol, at first as a way to tap into creativity, but his use evolved into addiction. His drug use got so bad he almost overdosed. Rehab saved his life. Fortunately, he grew up in an environment where he developed a strong willpower and it served him to get clean. Yet people would say things like, "his music was way better when he was high all the time."

After a few hours, the plane from Bombay landed in Dehradun. His agent had told him that someone would be there to pick him up. A young man said hello, asked to hold his bag for him, and then escorted him to the car in silence. After a thirty-minute drive from Dehradun, they arrived in Rishikesh—the birthplace of yoga. They entered a narrow road where street vendors lined both sides. Staring out of the window, A-Luv saw everything from clothes, fruits, vegetables, and street food being sold on the side of the street. Swarms of people were all around. The car moved slowly as the crowd naturally parted thanks to repeated honks. *Man, they sure do love to use the horn out here.*

In the middle of all the hustle and bustle. the car pulled up to a gate. The driver got out of the car, opened the gate, and then got back in to pull the car into a huge dirt lot with a single car garage. He parked the car in front of the garage, backed out a scooter, and pulled the car in. After closing the garage, he got on the scooter and started it, and motioned for A-Luv to sit on the seat behind him.

A-Luv asked the driver, "Are you for real? You want me

to sit behind on you this tiny ass scooter with a bag on my lap?"

They scooted back out onto the narrow street among all the vendors and people. The road wound down to Laxman Jhula, or bridge. The suspension bridge was barely wide enough for two lanes of people to walk on it. The Ganges River, which people from the area called *Gangama* or mother Ganges, flowed under the bridge. Watching the Ganges' emerald green power flow from the base of the Himalayas, A-Luv instantly felt a different vibe.

The driver inched the scooter onto the bridge and drove slowly. People whooshed around them as flowing water does around rocks. There were people taking pictures on the bridge, cows were walking on it, and families of monkeys dangling and playing on the suspension cables.

At the end of the bridge was a small pedestrian pathway lined with a temple, hotel, and stores. At the start of the path, the driver pulled up and stopped the scooter. He motioned for A-Luv to get down and opened the door to the store. A-Luv looked around in amazement—it was the jewelry shop his agent mentioned. He saw the driver take off his shoes, so he followed suit, then walked toward the back of the shop, where he saw a jolly man with neatly combed black hair and a thick mustache.

LIVE BEYOND YOUR IMAGINATION

"Welcome! Come, sit down," the man said in a deep and caring voice. A-Luv took a seat in front of the display case that separated the two of them. "Hi, nice to meet you. You must be Guddu. Your nephew speaks highly of you and arranged for me to come see you. His words were, you'd hook me up!"

"Very nice to meet you too! How has your trip to India been so far?"

A-Luv shook his head in amazement. "Man, it's definitely been a trip!"

Suddenly, a loud booming laugh came out, "AH ah ah ah ah ah ah ah!" It was one of those contagious laughs, and A-Luv found himself laughing along.

A-Luv finally continued, "The concert in Bombay felt incredible. The people gave me so much love and I loved feeling part of them. I haven't been to India since I was a little kid, and it's way different than I remember or expected it to be. I guess that's what I wanted. Something different, something out of my comfort zone, but also something meaningful."

He paused for a moment to see what reaction he'd get from Guddu, but instead of saying anything, Guddu sat there with a smile on his face, a sparkle in his eye, completely and totally present.

It made A-Luv more open than he expected to be. "I've been blessed with a lot of success in my life and I've come from nothing. I sort of feel guilty because I should be happy, but I'm not. I mean, I am sometimes, but I'm not at other times. And I don't really know how to fix that. Anyhow, I figured I'd do this concert in Bombay, and when Rohan told me to come to see you, I figured getting some bling wouldn't hurt."

Guddu said, "You see, that is why you are here. My nephew sent you for this very reason. But not for jewelry, no. You are here to learn the high vibe lifestyle. I will show you the five secrets of living each day with the kind of inner peace and freedom that allows you to be free from limitations to live a life way beyond your imagination. There are two conditions: First, you must stay here for the next three months. Give me three months, and I'll give you your life. Second, you must share these secrets with the rest of the world after you learn them. Not everyone will journey here, so you must allow this wisdom to flow you through to help others. Deal?"

Guddu's offer was different than the jewelry A-Luv was expecting to buy, but he was intrigued. He loved the feeling of adventure, and he thought this could be a relaxing vacation. He didn't have any obligations. Why not?

"Deal. So what's the first secret?"

"AH ah ah ah ah ah ah ah!! First, let us enjoy some chai, and tomorrow we will begin."

AWAKEN
YOUR SOUL

2

WOKE SOUL

A-Luv woke up to a bell ringing and chanting outside his room. He opened the door to his room in Guddu's house and saw a man in a robe performing some sort of ceremony around burning incense in a temple. A-Luv's mind started chattering with a Biggie verse:

"Who the heck is this? Wakin' me at 5:46 in the morning, crack of dawn and now I'm yawning, wipe the cold out my eye. See who's this waking me and why?" Why is he here, why did he wake me up, I was sleeping so well? That mattress was a little stiffer than the one at home. I wonder what time it is back home; this must be some sort of ceremony. I wonder what it does and what he's saying—is he hired or does he just go to everyone's house? He probably gets donations. Dinner last night was great; I'm a little hungry but I'll get ready first, then I'll go downstairs for breakfast. I wonder if Guddu is awake already? He probably is, who can sleep through this noise? Well, he's used to it so maybe he's asleep.

As he was showering, he heard loud chanting and clapping coming from the prayer room. This time, it was a different voice. He wondered who it could be now.

He got ready and left the room and peeked inside to find Guddu seated cross-legged on the floor, his body rocking back and forth in unison to the beat created by his claps, and singing something that was definitely off-key. He understood not to interrupt so he headed downstairs and sat at the kitchen table.

One of the helpers brought him freshly squeezed juice with what looked like some spice. She put the glass in front of him with a spoon, so he picked it up and stirred, having no idea what it was. As he took a sip, he tasted a delicious mixture of sweet juice with a salty kick. He put it down, taken back, trying to figure out what made the drink taste so mouthwatering.

Guddu sat down next to A-Luv and belted out, "Good morning! How are you?"

A-Luv described how he had heard chanting the morning and how he had looked to see who it was before he got ready to come downstairs.

Guddu smiled patiently and said, "So that is the second time you've told that story. The first time was in your head as it was happening, no?"

"Yeah, actually, my mind was racing."

Guddu explained how the mind loves to chatter. "It is always talking, never shuts up. It recreates the outside world inside yourself, which gives you the illusion of control. As long as you feel the need to protect yourself from life, your mind will keep narrating it as a protection mechanism. The world is unfolding and has very little to do with you. You must understand that you are not those thoughts. You are the observer of those thoughts. Try right now and listen to what those thoughts are saying."

A-Luv sat quietly and his mind began racing. *What am I supposed to do, the mind doesn't just stop, that's crazy, does he have any idea what he's talking about?*

"Now stop. Tell me what you witnessed and who witnessed it." A-Luv explained what he heard in his head and suddenly it was clear. He had observed his mind. If he was aware of what the mind was saying, then who was he to observe it?

"You see," said Guddu, "you are the one who is aware of the mind. When you are aware that you are aware, you've touched your soul. This brings me to the first secret: **Awaken Your Soul.**

"You must awaken your soul and let it be your guide. Today, go spend some time at Gangama. Just walk directly outside our house, down those stairs, and you will find a very comfortable place to sit and observe. I want you to take a seat and then close your eyes for a short while. Open them for three seconds and then close them again. Keep your eyes closed and describe to yourself everything you saw in as much detail as possible. Come to the shop when you're done."

After they finished breakfast, A-Luv headed down the stairs to sit in front of Gangama. He sat down and closed his eyes for a minute. He opened his eyes for three seconds and then closed them. For the next twenty minutes, he went into excruciating detail to describe in his head everything he saw. The color of the water, how fast it flowed, how wide the river was, the size of the rocks on the banks, and everything else in between. He opened his eyes and remarked to himself:

Wow, I was actually pretty dead on. I got the water color right, it's definitely flowing at the speed I recalled, the river's actually a little wider than I imagined, I wonder how long it would take someone to swim across it, those rocks are huge and the writing on them looks like Indian graffiti, I didn't describe those exactly how they are but I've never seen letters like that, reminds me of the first time I saw graffiti painted on a wall in the motel, it looked cool to me, I'm glad I never got into tagging, music definitely saved me from that, ok it's time make a move back to Guddu's shop, let's go.

He got up when he was done, walked to Guddu's shop, and removed his shoes at the entrance.

Guddu asked, "So, how did it go?"

"I'm actually really good at observing and describing details. I observe the world and write lyrics about it, so I felt like I was in my zone. I described pretty much everything. When I opened my eyes, there were a couple of things I would've added, but for the most part, I got it all."

Guddu responded, "Very good! Did you notice that with a single glance you were instantaneously aware of everything, and in high definition? Without any effort at all, you were aware of all the objects that were within the scope of your vision both near and far. Without having to move your eyes, your head, you could see details in things, perceive the different colors variations of light, the flow of the water, the width of the river, and any people around. Be aware of how you notice this all at once without having to think about it. Not a single thought was needed."

A-Luv was amazed, he was right. But what did that mean?

"Just as easily as you were able to look outside and see all the things, eventually you'll be able to sit deep enough within yourself to observe with your soul everything in front of you as well as your thoughts and emotions, rather than your mind. That place where you sit is your soul seat. Through your soul seat, you're aware of the thoughts, emotions, and the world pouring through your senses. You're able to see everything pass in front of you without getting lost. When you're watching the outer and inner objects of life go by, you're awake. That is spirituality. That is your soul. That is who you really are."

They sat in silence, and it didn't seem to bother Guddu one bit. A-Luv could hear the voice in his head start up again. *I wonder what he's going to say next? Should I try to make conversation, or would that be disrespectful?* And just then, it hit him. He was observing his thoughts and laughed. And as he laughed, Guddu gave a silent, close-lipped smile, in peace.

After a while, A-Luv couldn't take it anymore, so he asked, "What do you think about when you're sitting here?"

"Nothing."

"Isn't an idle mind the devil's workshop, though?"

Guddu replied, "When I find my mind is having wrong thoughts, I begin to chant a mantra quietly inside. Then the mind has no ability to focus on anything else. Eventually it passes, and I go back to having no thoughts."

"What's a mantra?"

"A mantra is a saying or a sound you repeat over and over in your head. It doesn't matter what it is, it can inspire you or just be a sound, but it will give your mind something to do till it gets quiet. Eventually, you will be able to sit in peace for hours, with no thoughts. That is a waking meditation. But that takes time and practice."

"No thoughts" was a way he would describe someone who was dumb, so A-Luv's b.s. radar went up. He was never one to mince words, so he hit Guddu straight on with what he thought.

"No disrespect, but having no thoughts sounds like someone who's slow. My mind is racing constantly. If my mind shut off, it's probably because I'm dead."

Guddu did not seem disturbed by A-Luv's comment and responded with clarity. "You have become so addicted to your thoughts that you can't separate your soul from your mind. The voice in your head constantly chattering comes from your ego. Your mind is playing tricks on you."

The Geto Boys' hook started playing in A-Luv's mind. *Tu tu ru ru tu tu tu tu, tu tu ru ru tu tu tu tu.*

EGO
vs
SOUL

"Can you imagine if your ego was an actual person? Pretend the ego is your best friend and is sitting right here on this seat next to you. You spend all your time with him, so of course he's your best friend. He would never stop talking and would describe everything he observed. He would give you advice, terrible advice, because he is biased. He would give you advice on something that disturbed him. He would try to tell you how to control the people around you. Here's the catch: you would listen to it all! You would get so caught up in his story and advice, you would lose yourself in the drama triangle."

A best friend who lives in your mind? This was new territory for A-Luv. Though he had been skeptical, he admitted Guddu made a lot of sense. The voice in his head said all kinds of things. Sometimes he listened and other times he didn't. He hadn't ever contemplated the ego and its chatter as a separate entity from his soul. But as he heard the words inside his head, "ego vs soul," he felt a truth.

"You mentioned a drama triangle. What's that?"

VILLAIN

VICTIM   HERO

"The drama triangle is where your ego lives. Think of it like the Bermuda triangle where planes disappear. When your ego is operating in the drama triangle, your soul disappears. Your ego is feeling one of three things: one, like a victim—someone or something is bothering him; two, like a hero—fine, I'll just do it myself and take care of it; or three, like a villain—you know what, let's see how they do without me.

"The drama triangle is not where your soul lives, though. Your soul sits in the center of your consciousness, outside the triangle. "

"So let me guess, if I want to act from my soul instead of my ego, I have to strengthen my soul."

"Correct!"

"Any chance you can tell me how?"

"Yes, of course. But first, you must understand energy."

"What's energy got to do with it?"

"You mean...what's *love* got to do with it?"

"Ohhhh! You did *not* just bust out some Tina Turner!"

"AH ah ah ah ah ah ah ah ah ah!! Very good, very good! You see how much energy you have right now? It is impossible not to laugh and feel anything but joy."

"I hear that!"

PREVENT ENERGY LEAKS

3

ENERGY LEAKS

Guddu's energy was contagious, and A-Luv knew how good he felt whenever he was with him, but he didn't quite understand why.

Guddu is such good people and I dig his vibe. And that laugh, dang, every time he laughs, he cracks me up! I don't even know why I'm laughing, but it sure does feel good. Maybe I don't laugh enough; I feel so heavy and serious most of the time, but with Guddu, I feel light and like a kid. I wonder what it is about him that gives off this vibe? He's definitely a super successful guy, but I get the feeling that his success is a result of the way he is. He's got this inner glow that feels pure and doesn't seem to depend on money. I wish I had that. I feel like if Guddu lost every penny, he'd still be laughing like that and it wouldn't phase him. He'd still have that type of joy no matter how rich or poor he was. How does he do it?

Guddu began with his next lesson. "We are all made up of energy. The first law of thermodynamics says energy is conserved. Energy cannot be created or destroyed—it can only be transferred. Nikola Tesla once said, 'If you want to find the secrets of the universe, think in terms of energy, frequency, and vibration.'

"Even when you get down to the atom, 99.9999999999999 percent of an atom is empty space filled with energy. If a proton was the size of an apple, the closest electron would be the size of a grain of salt, and it'd be roughly 1.24 miles away. That same energy is in everyone and is in everything. We're literally all made from the same energy source."

"Ok, that just blew my mind, in more ways than one." A-Luv always believed societies' race and gender inequities were superficial and had nothing to do with who people really were. He always believed everyone was the same inside, but that it was just an expression. Little did he realize the expression was factually true. Everyone is made of energy, which means we're all the same inside, and connected. The one thing he never heard before was that energy couldn't be created, that it could only be transferred.

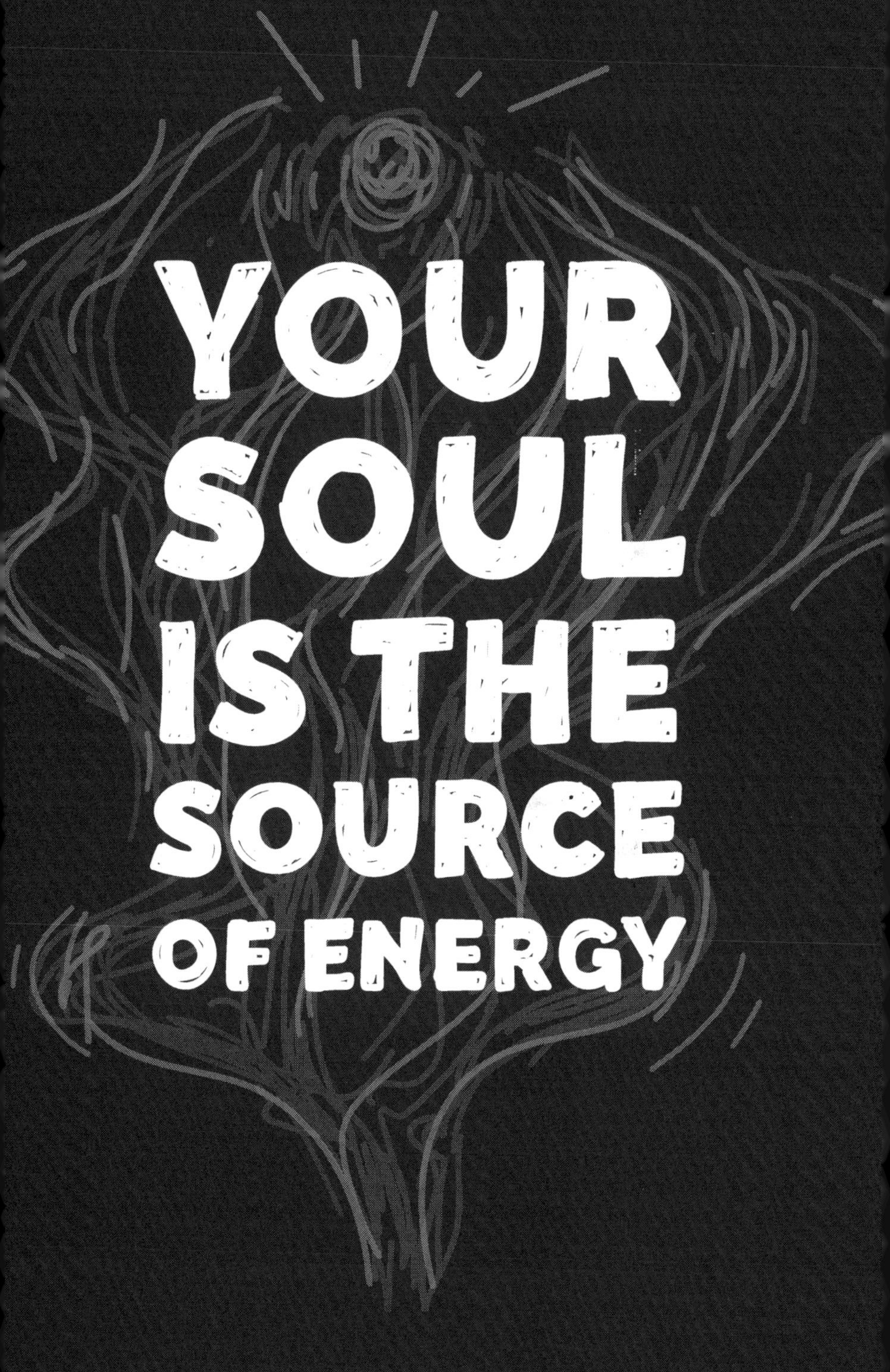
YOUR SOUL IS THE SOURCE OF ENERGY

"So whenever people say 'I gotta recharge,' we're not really creating energy?"

"No, we are not creating it. We are restoring the natural energy that's already there. This is why sleep and meditation are so crucial. You need to destress the body in order to stop energy leaks from happening."

"What causes energy leaks?"

"Very simple: one, unresolved conflicts; two, people; and three, things. Each of those triggers thoughts and emotions, which require a tremendous expenditure of energy."

"Can you explain each of those to me?"

"Certainly. Unresolved conflicts are the worst energy leak because there is an issue you never resolved within you. Imagine you are having dinner at a friend's house and the friend's aunt is in town from New York. At the end of the night she makes a joke at your expense and it embarrasses you. You don't address your embarrassment with the aunt or let it go, so the embarrassment remains unresolved in you. Now every time you talk to your friend, it triggers the pain from the aunt's joke. Anytime someone talks about an aunt or New York, you're triggered to feel pain. There is a ripple effect and you unknowingly and unwantedly leak energy.

"People and things can cause energy leaks too. Have you experienced people who drain you? Of course you have. Sure, sometimes people drain your energy because they are going through a hard time. That is temporary and you can give them energy to get through that. But if they are permanently that way, you can be kind but not allocate energy to them. Evaluate who you spend time with and reallocate your time to those who give you energy, or at least keep you neutral."

Growing up, A-Luv learned the value of loyalty. He felt he was expected to stay loyal to friends who had been with him since day one, but there were a couple who always took energy from him. Guddu helped A-Luv realize how certain people were draining his energy. After talking with Guddu, he felt he had permission not to give energy without totally dissing the person.

"And what about things?" A-Luv inquired.

WE'RE ALL MADE FROM

THE SAME ENERGY SOURCE

"Things are both material things and experiences. There is an expression, 'don't buy things, buy experiences.' Experiences are still bought. When you have things, you become attached to them. Imagine if I threw your phone into the river, how would you feel? You'd likely be angry or upset, and would expend a lot of energy being upset with me. Now imagine I threw my own phone into the river. You'd probably think I'm strange, but you wouldn't really care. No energy would leak. You see, emotional attachments to things causes us to lose energy. The more things you have, the more things you care about. The more things you care about, the more energy is leaking from your body. The fewer things you have, the less energy you drain. This is, in fact, why monks give up all their possessions when entering a monastery. Not because they renounce material things, but because the removal of things from their life allows them to store energy that they use for prayer and meditation. Keep only things that bring you energy and joy, and get rid of the rest, for it causes you to leak energy unnecessarily."

"I think I'm starting to get what you mean about energy not being created but being restored and how those three things leak energy from you," said A-Luv. "When I was working on my last album, it took everything out of me. To top it off, my girlfriend left me in the middle of making the album. I fell into a deep funk and I didn't want anything to do with anything. Then one day she calls me out of the blue and says how sorry she is, that she messed up, and that she wanted to see me that night. You know how fast I got ready? She was like, hang on a second, someone's at the door. I was like, 'It's me!' Where did all that energy magically come from and why don't I always have it?"

Guddu was impressed—now they were getting somewhere. "This energy comes from your soul. Your soul is the source of energy that pours into you, and that's what you're experiencing when you're excited about something and energy rushes up inside of you.

"The only reason you don't feel this all the time is because you block it by closing your heart. When you are closed, there is no light. There is no energy. There's nothing flowing into your soul. You actually have seven energy centers in your body known as chakras. One of them is the heart chakra. When energy is blocked in you, you get drained."

"So how do you stay open?" asked A-Luv.

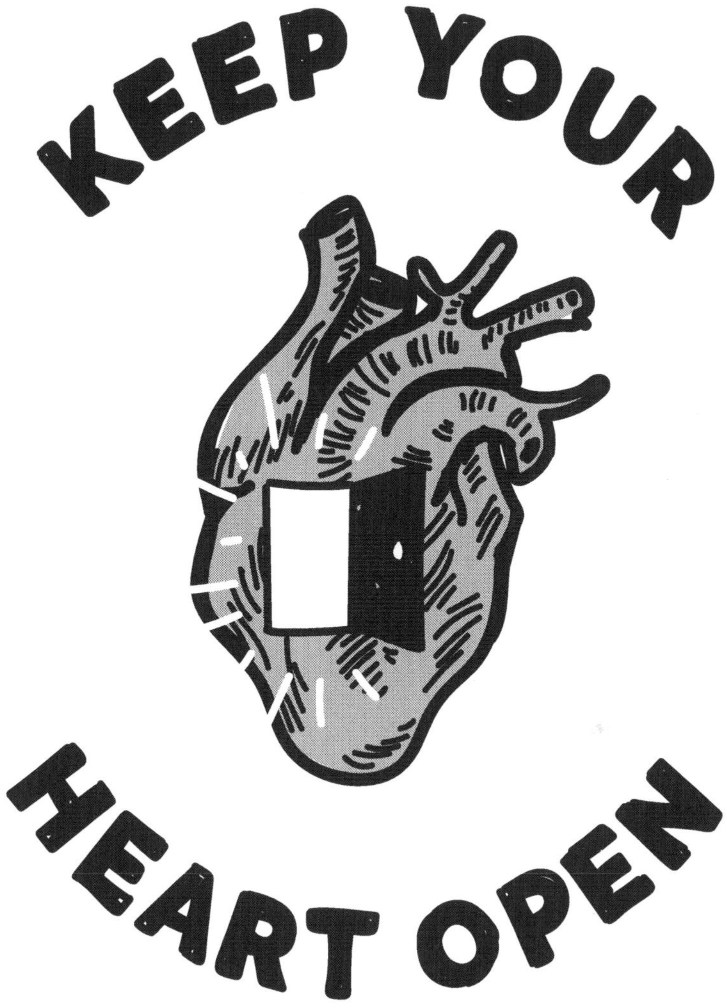
KEEP YOUR
HEART OPEN

"How does any restaurant stay open? They never close. All you have to do is decide if you're willing to stay open no matter what and train yourself to never close.

"That's why unresolved conflicts drain your energy. They cause you to close up. If your openness is determined by past experiences, then you're only going to be open if you have had a positive experience. You'll close up if the experience was negative."

"So basically, closing my heart doesn't really protect me from anything. It just cuts me off from getting some of that good juju flowing into me."

"Yes, that is right! Stay open no matter what happens. If you do, you get what everybody else is struggling for: love, enthusiasm, excitement, and energy. The more open you are, the more energy that will start to flow into you, and eventually so much energy will be flowing in you that it will flow out of you. People will actually start to feed off of your energy.

"Have you ever met someone who, when you talk to them, leaves you feeling full of energy? That's because they hold their vibe at a certain level and bring yours up. That's where the energy transferred.

"Energy can also help heal your body. The more energy

you allow into the system, the more your body can heal. That's why love can heal.

"Life is meant to be fun, and you should be excited to live it each and every moment. That's why the most important thing in your life is your inner energy. If you're inspired and filled with energy, then every minute of every moment is exciting. Learn to keep your energy centers open through meditation, relaxing, and releasing.

"Don't buy into the idea that something is worth closing over. If you love your life, nothing is worth closing your heart over. You must learn to let things go or else your heart will close."

Out of nowhere, Guddu's eyes darted to the entryway of the shop. "I see your shoes there. What kind are those?"

"Ah, those are the OG Nikes: Nike Cortez."

"They look very nice and shiny white. As you go around to explore today, make sure you return here with your shoes just as they are now. They should not be any dirtier than they are now and since they are brand new, they should come back today looking as such. Enjoy and I'll see you back here later this afternoon. Anytime is fine."

A-Luv walked to the entryway, where there were a number

of shoes and sandals. He put on his new kicks and before stepping out of the shop, he scoured the road.

Whoa it's like a river of people, there are just so many people. How are they not phased at those cows walking around? There's literally cow dung on the ground and no one's tripping. Let that cow ish get on my shoes and see what's up. Shoot. I'm not even playing. But these people are walking so fast, they're definitely going to scuff my kicks. I'm just gonna keep my head down and block people out with my arms and body like Shaq in the paint. Man I love Shaq. Shaq Diesel. That fool did a rap song. Supercalifragelistic, Shaq is alidocious. I wonder if he'd wanna collab with me?

YOU CAN'T CONTROL
THE OUTSIDE

TO PROTECT
WHAT'S INSIDE

Within seconds, it was clear that he was going to need to watch where he walked. He spent his time looking down at the walkway and path in front of him, walking around puddles of water, ducking and dodging whenever somebody would walk by and splash, walking around cow dung, stepping very carefully down the stairs toward the Ganges to make sure he didn't scuff them along the way. He spent the whole day building his life around the shoes. He felt exhausted after a few hours. When he went back to the shop, he came in with a solemn face because he knew that as hard as he had tried, the shoes didn't stand a chance of holding up. He took off his shoes in the entryway.

"So, how did your shoes hold up?"

A-Luv responded that as hard as he tried, he just could not prevent them from getting messed up. Guddu smiled and simply said, "That is okay, that was a very difficult task. How was the rest of your day?"

"I barely even noticed anything all day because I was focused on making sure that my shoes stayed clean. I just realized that I forgot to eat lunch and didn't talk to anyone. All I did was worry about the shoes."

"Did it occur to you that when you were leaving the store, there were a pair of sandals right next to your shoes?"

Guddu asked. "You could have taken off your socks and used those sandals for the entire day. If you were willing to let go of your shoes for the day, you would have experienced the day instead of being worried about your shoes.

"These shoes are everywhere, not only protecting your feet but protecting everything in you that you don't want to let go of. Instead of letting go of those things, you construct a life that does everything to protect your shoes from getting dirty, and if someone dirties them, you get angry at them, when all you had to do was take off your shoes.

"You don't need to get better at playing external games to protect what's inside. What you'll see is that your mind is always telling you that you have to change something outside in order to solve your inner problems. But if you are wise, you won't play this game. You realize that your mind's thoughts are tainted because your mind's thoughts are disturbed by fears. Of all the things you don't want to listen to, you don't want to listen to the advice of a disturbed mind.

"Your ego is constantly making demands of you, and you've devoted your life to serving those demands. If you want to be free, you have to learn to treat your ego like an addiction. When you have an addiction to alcohol, for example, you're capable of stopping yourself from drinking. It's not easy, but you are capable. In that same way, you are capable of not listening to the constant chatter from your ego. When you do that, your life is like a vacation. Everything is fun, family is fun, work is fun, wherever you are you are having fun. You actually live life instead of fearing or fighting it.

"Just realize that your mind is not qualified nor capable of getting you to stop. The mind is the problem, so you must go beyond the mind to detach from your ego. Stop expecting the mind to fix everything inside of you. The key is to be quiet. It's not that your mind has to be quiet. You be quiet. You, the one who was watching from the inside, just relax. Now, let's have some chai!"

THE MIND WON'T FIX

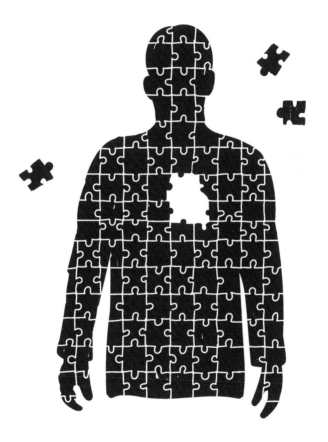

EVERYTHING INSIDE YOU

Guddu got up from behind the display case and A-Luv followed. They put on their shoes only to take a step outside and then enter a door directly adjacent to the shop, the entry to a hotel. They climbed up four flights of stairs and when they reached the top, they entered a restaurant and cafe that took A-Luv's breath away. Large floor to ceiling windows overlooked the Ganges, with a view of Laxman Jhula, the footbridge he had crossed to get there.

"Beautiful, isn't it? Come, sit down." A moment later, a waiter entered with two cups of chai.

A-Luv asked, "Do you have a tab here?" and Guddu roared with laughter.

"AH ah ah ah ah ah ah ah ah!! This is our hotel. We have so many visitors from all over the world coming to see us, so we built this hotel for them to have a place to stay."

"Wait, are you for real?"

"Yes, think how incredible the universe is that it gave us this hotel. When I first came here as a fifteen-year-old, I used to work there on that bridge as a photographer."

"Oh, so you moved here when you were in high school. What was that like?"

"I did not move here. My story is actually quite incredible to see how I got here. You see, I ran away from home when I was fifteen. I took a vase from my parent's house and left. I went to see a friend and said I wanted to go somewhere, and he said his father was stationed in the army in Rishikesh. So before we set off, I sold the vase for $1.50, and that is what I had in my pocket. We stayed for a week with his father and then my friend had to go back home. I said I was staying here, and though I had run out of money, I found my way.

"I started across the bridge where you entered and sold street food. I could eat and drink, and I found that to be enough. Then I thought one day, 'I've studied English in school, why don't I try to take photos of tourists on the bridge?' So I began to work with a photographer as his assistant and we did very well because I could talk to foreigners. Eventually, I saved up enough money to buy my own camera. I got married and we lived in a very small place where our three kids were born.

"Just across from my apartment was an elderly man who sold gemstones and jewelry. He was a very fine man and he treated me like a son. Each day he would come over and eat with us as a father would. He didn't have a family of his own, so we became family. I called him *Maharaji,* meaning prince. One day, he told me I should begin selling jewelry, but I thought, 'come on, I don't know a thing about this.' He said he would teach me, but I resisted. I was happy in life and didn't wish to make a change. One fine day while I was taking pictures on the bridge, a monkey snatched my camera and threw it off the bridge. Just like that, I was out of business!

"Ah ah ah ah ah ah ah ah ah ah!! I said 'ok, then I will start doing this jewelry business.'"

"Wait, so you just opened up a showroom and started selling high-end jewelry?"

"No no, it was not so easy. I did not have money to buy inventory, so Maharaji allowed me to take some inventory on credit, and he taught me. It turns out I have a good eye, a talent I was given. I had just a small table and was selling gemstones, but my gems were always certified and of the highest quality, and I always set a fair price. I never bargain. Slowly-slowly, I grew the business and had the inspiration to open a showroom. There was nothing here like it, but I had been given the calling, so I answered. I did my level best and that is the showroom you were in.

"After I opened the showroom, I had another inspiration: to build a house here on this street. You won't believe it—I didn't have the money to build it! I just got the inspiration one day and started construction. The moment I ran out of money, customers would buy something from the shop and a large sum of money would come in to pay for the next step of construction. On and on that went until our house was built. That is the house you are staying in and it is still the only one on this road.

"You see, I never took any tension. I always saw what was happening in the outside world with an understanding that it does not affect my inner joy. Just like we sit up here and observe the river and people below, that is how I see myself. I simply observe."

"So does that mean you don't really do anything, that it all just comes to you?"

"Of course not! That is lazy. When one gets called to do something, you must work hard, be honest, and use your brain to be very smart."

"I don't get it. How can you be chill and driven at the same time? It seems like those are opposites."

"This is a very good question, and your timing is perfect. You see the black Scorpio down there, that is for us. Your bag is already packed and in the back. For the next few months, you'll learn meditation. You will learn skills to actually make meditation stick. Too many people think they begin with meditation and that is why they are unable to do it. You must learn the skills first, only then can you meditate. And once you are able to meditate, it is a portal into your consciousness. There, you will find the answer to your question. *Chalo,* let's go."

CHANGE
FOR YOU

4

CHANGE
FOR YOU

As they got into the SUV, A-Luv wondered how this large SUV actually got into the small strip where scooters could barely make it across the bridge. They began driving down a road overlooking the Ganges.

Staring out the window, A-Luv observed the water flowing in the opposite direction as they traveled upstream. They passed ashrams with steps leading down to the water and some campsites. They continued driving for fifteen minutes surrounded by jungle on both sides until they pulled up to Guddu's yoga retreat center and exited the car.

Ahhh, this place is beautiful and the vibe here is so peaceful. That's funny, I just realized I didn't even have to describe the whole place to myself. My consciousness took it all in within an instant. Dang, that's cool. It's working! Ok slow down Husain Bolt, you're still learning.

Guddu and A-Luv were greeted by the reception staff with a *namaskar,* palms together in front of the chest and a small bow. A young, radiant woman walked from behind the reception desk. She stood no taller than 5' 2" but she exuded such positive energy that it made A-Luv pause. She had long, black, shiny hair, perfect skin, big and inviting light brown eyes, a small red jewel in the center of her forehead, and a warm, bright smile. She wore a fitted white top that went down past her waist, thin baggy white pants, an ornate bead necklace, and a light orange type of scarf draped around her neck.

She smiled at A-Luv and welcomed him. Then she did something A-Luv hadn't seen since he was a kid; she bowed down from her waist and touched Guddu's feet with her hands. In return, Guddu touched the top of her head and said, "*Khush raho, bless you.*" Guddu and the woman spoke for a minute in Hindi. A-Luv understood Hindi pretty well since his parents spoke it growing up. Guddu was clear in his instructions and his tone was fair but firm. He could tell right away that Guddu didn't play when it came to business. Then he said, "Let me introduce you to Nikki. She is an absolute angel. When she came to visit me many years ago, I knew she was one-of-a-kind. Such a kind soul and full of love. Incomparable."

Out of respect, she added *ji* to the end of his name, a suffix used in honor. "Gudduji is too kind. He saw in me what I did not know was there. I came to him for jewelry and ended up staying here for many months to learn the high vibe lifestyle. Now I stay here year-round and help others with their practice."

"She does much more here as well. She runs all our teacher trainings year-round, and she hosts our annual summit. As you walk the grounds with Nikki, you will see people from all over the world here. Hundreds of them. And in just a few weeks, there will be a big celebration.

"*Chalo*, have a look around with Nikki and then come join us for some chai."

"Sounds like you run the show around here. Had you ever run something like this before?"

"Oh my goodness, no. I'm originally from Hyderabad and came out here for a spiritual journey. Some friends had come to Laxman Jhula and they met Gudduji, in search of spiritual jewelry. They ended up staying for a few months and when they returned, I could hardly recognize them. Not that they looked different, but they just had a glow about them—a vibe that made me feel great just being near them."

I know what you mean about their vibe making you feel great being near them. I felt like that the instant I saw you. I feel a little weird admitting this to myself, but I got all the feels. I mean you're attractive, for sure, but it's more than that. Whenever you say something in that dulcet voice, you lift my energy.

MEDITATION IS A PORTAL

INTO YOUR
CONSCIOUSNESS

"So I made my plans to come out here, and when I did I quickly realized that this wasn't just a trip for spiritual jewelry. Guddu saw that I was suffering inside even though on the outside, I looked to have it all. Inside, I suffered from insecurity and I had a bit of a hot temper too. He made it his mission to share with me the high vibe lifestyle."

"Whaaat?! No way you've got a temper. You seem like the most chill person. Do you still get heated like that?"

"Not anymore, and that's thanks to what Gudduji taught me about meditation. I learned a couple of meditation practices that really stuck and use those tools at every moment. It's made me the version of myself who I love and, not to mention, those same tools help me run this yoga retreat center.

"Come, let me show you around, and I'll share with you the lessons I've learned."

"Well, I gotta warn you, I don't really sit still so well, and my mind is always racing. I've tried a couple of meditation apps, but it felt silly just sitting there and basically thinking the whole time. I don't think meditation is for me, so just giving you a heads up—I don't want you to get your hopes up."

"All good, I totally understand, as I was exactly the same way, too. The five foundational steps are the reason meditation stuck with me. Most people think meditation is the starting point and that's when you lose. That'd be like saying you wanted to be a doctor, so you start in med school. You have to do pre-med first."

"So this is like pre-meditation?!"

"Haha, yes, that's exactly right!"

"Well, I'm game. I listen to a ton of podcasts and almost every person I admire has meditation as a common denominator. At first, I thought the first couple people were frontin' but then when it kept coming up over and over again, I was like yo, maybe this is for real."

They came upon a beautifully manicured garden. There was a colorful diversity of vibrant flowers and plants, the sound of water flowing, and a spectacular view of the Himalayas and the Ganges. A-Luv stopped to take it in.

"This is our meditation garden. Come, let's have a seat as this is the perfect place to share the five foundations of meditation." They walked down a path and came upon a meditation nook, where they sat next to each other. Their knees touched when they sat, and A-Luv felt a bolt of electricity shooting through his body.

"Whoa. Did you feel that?"

"I did," Nikki said with a coy smile. "What did it make you feel?"

"Honestly, it feels like there's some chemistry between us but not in a sexual way. Like you're super-hot and all, but it feels different."

You're super-hot?! Why did you just say that? That's when you lost, son. Or maybe she liked it. I don't know, I'm straight up confused. I need to spit game at this girl. What? No, that's a terrible idea. That's not why you're here. Why am I feeling so confused? Actually, maybe that's the ego that Guddu was telling me about. Maybe the ego is the one telling me I need to holler at her, and my soul is telling me otherwise.

CONTROL
YOUR

AWARENESS

"What do you think we felt?" asked A-Luv after letting a few awkward seconds pass.

"I don't label it. I just am aware that I felt something too. And that's the first foundation: **control your awareness.**

"Let's try something so you can experience for yourself exactly how awareness can be controlled. Close your eyes and keep them closed this whole time. I'm going to ask you questions but you don't need to answer them out loud. Say the answer to yourself without speaking.

"Now become aware of what's around you. What can you hear?" *I hear the Ganges water flowing over the rocks. I hear birds chirping. I hear the wind. I hear you breathing.*

"Can you feel the bench under your seat?" *I sure can. It's strong and sturdy.*

"Now turn your awareness to the inside of your body. Can you feel the warmth in your body?" *Yeah, I've never thought about it that way before. I know when I feel warm, but haven't ever tried to feel the warmth in my body. But yeah, I can feel the warmth. Come to think of it, there's a really subtle tingling feeling that's warming my body.*

"Now think back to your last vacation. Where did you

go?" *Turks and Caicos.* "Where did you stay?" *Grace Bay.* "What was the weather like when you arrived?" *It was sunny and a little humid but felt like paradise. Exactly what I was wanting. Blue skies, a few clouds overhead, and a faint wind.*

"Picture one of the outfits you wore during the day. What did you have on top?" *Nothing, I was shirtless most of the day trying to get my tan on.* "What did you have on bottom?" *Navy blue board shorts with some bright flowers.* "Did you have anything on your head?" *I was rocking a flat bill, New Era hat.* "What type of shoes were you wearing?" *I had some Havaianas flip flops on.*

"Now think back to the day you landed in India. What did you see when you first landed?" *I saw a bunch of people. Like huge mobs of people and no lines. Felt like everyone was doing whatever they wanted.*

"What were you wearing then?" *I was rocking my all-white Nike Cortez, jeans, an original Gucci shirt from back in the day, a black bomber jacket with gold zippers, and a flat bill, New Era hat.*

"How did you get from the airport to wherever you were staying?" *I had a car waiting for me. The dude had a sign with my name on it. I was expecting a big luxury car because my agent knows how I roll, but I ended up in a small car. Well,*

I guess it was bigger than the other cars on the road, but it felt like I was rolling in a jelly bean.

"Now bring your awareness back to the inside of your body. Can you again feel the warmth?" *I can.*

"Does it feel any different?" *A little bit more tingly now. I can definitely still feel the warmth pouring out my skin.*

"Now bring your awareness back to your surroundings. What do you hear and feel?" *Yeah, I can hear the Ganges river again. I can feel the slight breeze in the air, and I hear this one bird chirping nonstop. I hear myself breathing.*

YOU GOT
GAME

"Go ahead and open your eyes now. What did you notice?"

"That was a trip! It felt like you were taking me on a journey but just with my mind."

"Not your mind..."

"Right! With my awareness. I transported to every one of those scenes just with my awareness."

"All those scenes exist within your mind. Think of them like rooms. Your mind doesn't move, it's fixed, and it has a bunch of different rooms in it. Your awareness is what moves and can travel room to room. When you go into a room, imagine you are holding a flashlight that, when you point it to a certain area of the room, you are able to see it and recall details. You strengthen that area of the mind every time you visit it so you must be careful where your awareness is at all times. You must be aware of your awareness. Those rooms are your subconscious and when you visit a room with your flashlight, you are bringing that to the conscious part of your mind, good or bad."

"So if I hear you right, anytime my awareness is stuck on something negative, I'm giving it energy and strengthening that negativity. I know I have some pretty unhealthy talk tracks running through my mind and every time that happens, I'm only making it harder to get rid of because it's getting stronger as more energy is feeding it."

"That's exactly right. You are in complete control of your awareness when you recognize that your awareness is getting into some negative areas of the mind. All you have to do is gently and lovingly bring your awareness to a positive area of your mind. I say gently and lovingly because you don't need to put yourself down for your awareness having gone to a negative place. Just be aware that it's there and move it somewhere else. What's an example of one of those negative talk tracks you mentioned that you go to on a daily basis?"

"There's one that hits me all the time: I'm not good enough. Literally, from the time I wake up in the morning and get dressed, I'm figuring out what bling to wear. It's like the chip on my shoulder moved to my wrist. Wearing a Rolly, chains, and rings is basically bedazzled armor for the front I'm putting up. I want people to know I'm rich and that I am good enough, because I don't believe it myself. Not all the time, but I definitely go there on a daily basis. I'll buy and do things just to fill that void, and then of course you know I gotta put it on the Gram so that people will tell me how good I am. If I don't get external validation and I'm left to my own inner monologue, I feel depressed because I feel like I should be doing more. Like even though I've had all this success, there's just so much more I should've done or should be doing. Damn, sorry to unload like that."

"There's a lot there, and I know that Gudduji's lessons to come will help you. But you'll learn those a little later. For now, I want you to come up with a replacement talk track, a positive place for you to move your awareness when this comes up. You can't eliminate head trash without changing your beliefs. I bet you have some really healthy and positive beliefs about yourself that simply need strengthening, and by moving your awareness there, away from the negative talk, you're giving less energy to the negative and giving more to the positive."

"Yeah, I'm glad we got to this point, because I'm not always feeling down on myself. I know I've been blessed with some incredible gifts in my life and I work my tail off to go after them. Even though I don't have to, I'm still one of the hardest-working rappers in the game. I put out albums consistently, do shows around the world, and help other rappers come up in the game. I know this about myself: I'm a h-u-s-t-l-e-r, hustler.

"So next time I find my awareness diving into that self-pity head trash about how I'm not good enough, I'm going to move my awareness to this part of my mind which knows I got game. But now that I think about it, I bet that's a lot easier to say than it is to do. Especially when I'm in a funk, I know that I can move my awareness, but I'm not sure how long I can keep it there without slipping back into the negative space."

"Well, let me first tell you, the ability to gently and lovingly control your awareness is exactly what you practice inside of meditation. When you're meditating, you'll find that your awareness is supposed to be on one thing and instead, it goes somewhere else. It's not your mind racing, it's your awareness constantly shifting.

"By picking something you do every day where you can practice redirecting your awareness, you'll build the foundational skills needed to be good at meditating. When you get to the point where you're ready to start meditating, you'll have the skills to control your awareness. Meditation will further hone these skills so they transfer into all aspects of your life. Come, let's stretch our legs and I'll show you around a little more."

They got up and walked leisurely out of the garden and into a construction zone. Nikki explained how they already had eighty-four rooms and still, so many people were coming to the retreat center it was completely booked. Guests were happily sleeping on the desks so they could stay. To accommodate the demand, they began constructing two new buildings to add fifty new rooms. They just finished building a grand yoga *shala,* or hall, where over 1,000 yogis could practice, because the two existing yoga shalas were simply not enough. A-Luv watched as Nikki spoke with such ease and clarity with her team as they walked the grounds. She was clearly a gifted organizer and leader of people, and she got stuff done.

They circled around one of the buildings and came upon a grassy area with a four-foot-tall black and gray Buddha statue adorned with orange and yellow marigold garlands and loose flowers amongst his head, hands, and feet. The statue sat atop a small podium where more flowers lined the front along with *diyas* and incense. A rock with *om* written on it sat in the middle. On the grass lay a magenta-colored cloth covered in gold flowers with three clay pots holding flowers and incense. To the Buddha's left was a smaller bronze statue of Shiva, also adorned with orange and yellow marigolds. Behind both statues, the Ganges formed a green cloak as if it were wrapping itself around the deities.

PRACTICE
CONCENTRATION

"Come, let's take a seat," she said, and they sat on the ground, cross-legged. "You mentioned earlier how when you're in a funk, you're not sure how long you can hold your awareness in a positive area of the mind before it slips back into a negative space. This brings us to the second foundation for meditation: **practice concentration.** Concentration is simply prolonged focus so when you are trying to hold your awareness in a positive area of the mind, this requires your energy to concentrate.

"Have you ever been in such deep concentration that time seemed to stand still? Nothing disturbed you and you were in a flow state?"

"Yeah, whenever I sit down to write lyrics or I'm in the studio making beats, I'm trying to get into that zone all the time. It doesn't always happen though, but when it does, it's like magic. That's actually why I like having no one around me when I'm writing—I need that time to concentrate, and I can't have people distracting me."

"So you already know the benefits of concentration and how much you can accomplish without distractions. But think about how good we are at distraction. Let me ask you, if someone came to you said they wanted to be a rapper, how many days a week would they need to practice?"

"I'd say every day, or at least six days a week and chill for one day."

"And how many hours a day would they need to practice?"

"I feel like they'd have to be writing, coming up with stories, and practicing at least ten hours a day."

"And after six months, would they be able to write a hit song?"

"Probably not."

"But they would be a lot better than when they started, is that right?"

"Yeah, for sure."

"Now how many days a week would you say *you* live with distractions? Where you are pulled in multiple directions."

"That's every day of my life."

"Right on. And how many hours in a day are you distracted? Maybe it's different people needing your attention, having multiple websites open, getting emails and texts and DMs?"

"Morning till night. At least ten hours a day, if not more."

"So if you practice distraction ten hours a day, six days a week, how good are you at managing distractions?"

"I'm great at it. I feel like my job is to multi-task and keep all these balls in the air."

"I imagine you're world-class at it, given how many years you've been practicing managing all the distractions in your life. That's the issue most people have. They are excellent at distraction and terrible at concentration. Let me ask you this, who taught you how to concentrate?"

"I don't think anyone ever taught me, really. I just do it when I can, and it's definitely not most of the time."

"You ever notice how parents and teachers are constantly telling kids to sit still, to focus, to concentrate, stop getting distracted? And yet, no one ever taught them how. This is why so many kids are medicated to calm down, when really, many would benefit by learning how to concentrate. Those kids grow up to be distracted adults, and we all know most innovation comes from concentrated energy."

"This makes total sense. When I was a kid, I used to run around everywhere, and my teachers said I was a distraction in class. I just had a bunch of energy and I started to hate school and especially teachers who were always criticizing me. Now they see me and they praise me for the energy that they felt was problematic.

MONKEY
MIND

"I remember carrying a notebook around with me and, matter of fact, I still do. I would write about what I saw, things people would say, and I'd write stories about my experiences. I even wrote some plays and poems. I sat for hours in my tiny room with a record playing, put pen to pad, and would write rhymes. Verse after verse. Once I had the idea that I was going to be a rapper, I put everything I had toward that goal. It kept me out of a lot of trouble on the streets too. It would have been a lot easier to kick it with my friends, sell dope, and make some money, but I had this internal strength to stay on course.

"It's never been like that after that first album, though. I went on tour and everything I ever wanted in life started coming my way—I had friends and fans everywhere, more money than I ever imagined, women and drugs for sure, and it's been like that ever since. So when I sit down to write songs now, I don't ever really have that much concentrated time where I'm focused."

"What you're describing is precisely what we're going to solve by teaching you how to concentrate. While you can remove external distractions, know your mind creates distractions for yourself as well. Meditation is not only about tuning out external distractions, it is also learning to tune out mental distractions by remaining concentrated. The mind is like a chattering monkey that never stops. A sound will pull your mind in one direction, you will have a thought, you feel a sensation in your body, you will have a thought. When you come to the point that you can tune out your senses and the world around you, then your mind will race to the past or the future. Your mind will try to distract you. The mind will keep talking unless you give it one thing to focus on. With practice your concentration will become so deep, the mind quiets, stops talking, and becomes silent. In your mind's silence you will find a deep sense of stillness and peace.

"So if you don't learn how to concentrate, you'll never be able to meditate and you'll not be able to call upon the ability to stay focused for prolonged periods of time when you need it."

"Hey, listen, if you can teach me how to get better at concentration and live less distracted, I'm all game."

"Great. Let's start with a simple exercise to see how long you're able to concentrate. You see this lit candle sitting here, I'd like you to stare only at the flame without blinking your eyes for as long as you can. I'll count in my head and if your eyes shift somewhere or you blink, then time's up. Ready? Begin."

A-Luv fixed his gaze on the flame and as he did, he became aware of where his awareness was going. Within seconds, his awareness shifted from *staring at this flame* to *look at the flame dancing, it's yellow by the wick but then goes clear.* Every time he observed his awareness shifting and his mind chattering, he brought his awareness back and refocused on just looking at the flame. And then he blinked.

"25 seconds. Not bad."

"Not good either. Let's go head to head, maybe I need some competition. The first one to blink or shift their eyes loses. Ready, go."

Nikki and A-Luv sat staring at the flame. Nikki sat with soft eyes and an unwavering focus, and A-Luv stared easily for a while till he felt the need to blink and his awareness could only think about not blinking. His eyes began to water, and he held them open like bug eyes. Until finally, he couldn't any longer and he blinked. The water that welled in his eyes from holding them open fell down his cheeks. He wiped the tears and rubbed his eyes and he said, "Man, I didn't even come close! But that second time around was way better, right?"

YOU CAN ACCOMPLISH ANYTHING WITH

WILLPOWER

"You sure are driven, I'll give you that! That was much better than your first time, and that's because you exerted much more willpower over yourself. With willpower, you can accomplish anything in life. By **strengthening your willpower**, you will strengthen your ability to hold your focus and thus, you'll be able to concentrate for longer periods of time."

"I feel like I used to have a ton of willpower. I thought of it more like self-discipline, but the idea sounds the same. It was a power I exerted over myself to do something, even when I wanted to do something else. When I wanted to go out with my friends after school, I exerted willpower and said 'No, if you want to make it in the rap game, you need to work on your lyrics.' So how do I get that back?"

"Simple, by finding everyday things to exert your willpower over. Just like we did with concentration, what's something you do every day that you could do just one percent better? For example, when you get up, do you make your bed? After you eat, do you wash the dishes and put them away?"

"Damn, I think I've gotten soft! I don't mess with anything anymore. I do whatever I have to but honestly, I do the bare minimum. I feel like so much of that stuff is beneath me."

"Don't think of something you *need* to do, think of something that will let you practice willpower. You're not cooking breakfast because you have to, for example— you're cooking breakfast so you can strengthen your willpower."

"I get you. Okay, let me think of something. Hmm, what's something I do every day that I could do a little better? I know, don't judge, but when I take a leak and it gets on the rim of the toilet, I just figure my housekeeper will clean it up. I could grab a piece of toilet paper and wipe it down."

"Hahahaha! Yes, perfect!!"

"I've never heard anyone so excited about me taking a leak before," A-Luv said with a smirk.

"And I want you to add one more thing to your bathroom routine to practice concentration. When you're done wiping the toilet rim and you're washing your hands, I want you to hold your focus on washing your hands. It's something you do many times a day without thought. Now, I want all your awareness to be held on the water running over your hands. If your awareness shifts, use your willpower to bring it back and hold it there. Over time, by doing more than you have to, you'll strengthen your willpower. By using your willpower to hold your focus, you'll strengthen your ability to concentrate. That will serve you well when you begin to meditate and will grow in strength. Imagine how easily you'll be able to call upon yourself to concentrate and how much you'll accomplish in that heightened sense of awareness."

VISUALIZATION BRINGS CLARITY

Guddu walked up behind them with a cup in each hand. "Helloooo. Here is your chai. I did not want it to get cold. Come, I want to show you something which I think you will like." Without missing a beat, Guddu turned and began walking with A-Luv and Nikki in stride. They came up to a small building that looked like it could be a guest house, but without windows. When they walked inside, A-Luv knew exactly where they were—in a studio. At the yoga retreat center was a full-service content creation building with racks of servers, huge monitors all around, audio-video equipment, and a recording booth.

"You built a studio??"

"You seem surprised! Ah ah ah ah ah ah ah ah ah ah!!!"

A-Luv walked around and peeked over the shoulders of the workstations where people were working, some in pairs and some alone. They had the newest hardware and software and when he stepped into the studio, he couldn't believe his eyes. There was a fully outfitted mixing room and recording room. In the recording room was a full instrument setup with drums, bass and electric guitars, keyboards, and numerous mic setups. There were also instruments he wasn't so familiar with. "What are those instruments called?" he asked Guddu.

"Let me show you. Go have a seat there in the mixing

booth." He motioned to a few people to come over, said something in Hindi, and they picked up the instruments and began playing. A-Luv had never heard anything like it. The elements of a Western band were all there, but it was like an Indian version of The Roots playing in front of him. There were two hand drums called *tablas*; a two-headed bass drum slung over the neck of a player, called *dhol*; a long-necked stringed instrument vaguely resembling a guitar, known as the *sitar*; and a bellows-driven keyboard on the floor called a *harmonium*. The music was magical.

"I've never heard anything like that. So much rhythm and bass, and the melodies are off the chain! I'm blown away right now. How did you put all this together? Why does this all exist here?"

"This is not something I even knew about, so it is funny how it all happened. Whenever people would come here, they would say 'Guddu, you need to share your message to people around the world, not only to those who come here.' That is why I told you one of my conditions was for you to share these lessons when you go back to the US. They told me that is not enough, that we must produce content and share it with the world. A few volunteers were passionate about this, as they were in the media and marketing business, and they felt they could help us. So I said *teak hai*, you do what you want and let me know what you need. One young man was a videographer, so he began filming, someone else was an editor, others were writers, and some were musicians. They all stay here now and work on these projects. Some of our films are on Netflix, our content is read worldwide, and we produce our own podcast and music. I didn't do any of this. It all came from the divine blessings of Gangama."

"But surely you helped these people to think this way and to give them the creative space to come up with ideas and produce them? This isn't all without your doing, right?"

"See. You are learning meditation and Nikki has taught you the first two skills: awareness and concentration. The next skill to learn will explain how this all came about. It's called **visualization**. When you learn to visualize properly, getting a clear mental picture helps you turn visualizations into reality. The problem is, most people are never taught how to visualize, so people who teach meditation don't include it. They instead ask people to focus on the breath, which is important for sustained focus, but there is never an intention or goal inside their meditations. This is missing the point. You must have a goal, or else why would you do it? You won't, because you won't receive anything back from practicing meditation."

"Yeah, I always thought meditation was supposed to be where you clear your mind. Now I know it's not about clearing the mind, it's about concentrating your awareness on the right place in your mind. I've never heard of having a goal inside of meditation, but that makes a lot of sense to me. Otherwise you're right, why would anyone stick with it? So how does one learn to visualize?"

That was Nikki's cue. As she heard the question coming out of A-Luv's mouth, she reached her closed hand out, gently pulled A-Luv's hand with her free hand and opened her fist to place some small items in his palm.

Whoa, another jolt of electricity just shot through me. Something is going on with Nikki, and I'm feeling so open and vulnerable. I should tell her what I feel. No, don't do that, that'll spook her. Fine, tell her something meaningful. Like what? Like about the fact that I would change for her. I'm already changing for myself, but now I realize that the changes are internal. I would change the external things about my life for you, if you feel for me the way I feel for you. Too far, reign it in a bit. Better yet, don't say anything. Just look at whatever she put in your hands.

When A-Luv looked down at his hand, he saw some of the most brilliant gems he'd ever seen. There in his hand was a diamond, an emerald, a ruby, a yellow sapphire, and a blue sapphire. Nikki lined them up in a row and said, "Take a look at the colors of each precious gemstone. Now close your eyes and picture only the diamond and hold that image for three seconds. *1-2-3.* Now think of the next gemstone in the order it's placed in your hand. Visualize that gemstone and hold it for three seconds. *1-2-3.* Continue until you visualize all five stones.

"Were you able to see them all in great detail?"

"Yeah, that was pretty easy."

"Great, let's try it again and this time, I'll change the order and you're going to hold the visual for thirty seconds each." Nikki rearranged the gemstones in his palm and called for A-Luv to visualize the first one all the way through the fifth one. "How did it go this time?"

"That was harder, actually. I could definitely see them, but my awareness would shift into something else and when I'd bring it back, the image had faded some."

"You see how hard it is for you to visualize five gemstones you've seen in real life for thirty seconds? Now you see why visualizing something that doesn't exist is even harder, but the more clearly you can see it, the easier it is to turn into reality. If you practice small visualizations and build your strength, you will be able to take on larger visualizations over time."

A-Luv handed the gemstones back to Nikki. He said to Guddu, "I actually think I do visualize some things pretty well but definitely not everything. Like when I'm going on tour and my team and I are working on the show, I definitely have a clear picture of what I want and how it should look that's all formed initially in my mind. The hard thing is getting everyone else to see the same thing."

"You are correct," Guddu said. "You definitely experience visualization, but you are not always seeing it in high-definition. You are seeing it in SD. So even though the picture is fairly clear to you, it takes time to get others to see it. By strengthening your visualization skills, not only can you bring more ideas to life, but you also gain tremendous clarity that helps you communicate your vision more effectively."

This sank in more than Guddu even knew. A-Luv conjured up example after example of when he was frustrated because he felt his creative control was slipping and people on his team would distort his vision. What if he pointed the finger to himself and asked, "But are you seeing this in HD or are you getting clarity while expecting others to have it?"

Nikki reappeared, having returned the gemstones. A-Luv asked, "So how do I strengthen my visualization skills so that I'm ready to apply it inside of meditation, and then to my life?"

"You see how we practiced on the gemstones?" Nikki said. "You can practice with anything for thirty seconds. Simply look at it for three seconds and close your eyes—your consciousness will absorb everything. Then hold the visual in your mind for thirty seconds. When you can do that with ease, you're ready to take on the two visualizations needed for meditation.

"The first is being able to see exactly how you are seated. You may need to look in a mirror at first. The second is to see the miles of nerves running throughout your body. You're going to utilize both of those in meditation, so best to get a visual of that beforehand."

A-Luv looked at the mirrors inside the mixing room just to get a picture of how he was sitting. It felt a little silly since he assumed he knew how he looked but he did pick up some nuances. The bend in his elbows and knees, and how his head was a little forward instead of directly over his shoulders. Out of the corner of his eye, he caught a glimpse of a Roland drum machine. "Hey, any chance I could play on that drum machine for a hot second? I just had a beat pop into my head that goes with the music they just played. I wanna see how it comes out."

He moved over to the drum machine and tapped on the pads. He pulled up some sounds on a laptop connected to the machine. As he tapped away, the elements began to emerge. First the 808 drums, then the melodies, and finally he layered in the baseline. As he tapped away and recorded each track, he assembled a beat. He asked the musicians to come back in and play what they played before. Four metronome taps started them off. When the music came in, it was like two lovers meeting after being apart for too long. It just worked. When the song finished, everyone felt it. No one said anything for a few seconds, basking in the afterglow. And then the silence was broken.

"*Arey wah!! Shabash, shabash!*" Guddu boomed. Everyone exploded into high fives and hugs and cheers!

"You see," Nikki said, "how you had a vision and turned that into a goal of making music to accompany the song? I can tell you were going by feel from there. You were feeling the music and how it would work together. It took you no time to move from vision to goal to feeling. This is the same process you will use inside of meditation. You start with a vision and turn that into a goal. And once you have that goal, you must concentrate on what it feels like to achieve that goal. Do not let your ego get in the way as it will try to creep in and distract you. Actually feel it throughout your body, in your nerves, in the energy coursing through you."

I am definitely feeling it. Whenever I get into a flow state, it's like nothing in the world is around me. It's just me. And the music is pouring through me so that I literally feel it in my body, in my veins, like it's rushing to get out. That's what just happened. I caught a vibe and could hear the sounds reverberating in my mind but also in my body. It's like I could actually feel the beat before it got laid down. I could hear the harmonies, I could hear what it needed and give it those sounds. I get your point now—when I have a vision and turn that into a concrete goal, the second I start to feel it, I'm gonna make moves and make it happen.

"That was dope. I was totally feeling it."

"Exactly, you were feeling it. Not imagining it, not sensing it. No. You were feeling it. When you are as concentrated in that feeling as you were just then, the path to making your vision a reality is quick. That is how this entire production studio was created. The students visualized it, set a goal, and felt it in every sinew in their body. When it came time to design and build, it happened in no time. This project normally takes eight to twelve months in India. Maybe four to six months in the US. It took us six weeks.

"Listen, why don't you take some rest and freshen up in one of the rooms. Nikki has already set it up for you. And after your nap, we can have dinner."

That was music to A-Luv's ears. As much as he wanted to spend time in the studio, he felt that he had learned so much and needed to absorb it all and restore some energy. When he got to the room, he crashed hard. He woke up a couple hours later to a light tap on the door. "Dinner is about ready. Wanna freshen up and meet me outside?" A-Luv felt rejuvenated and excited to see Nikki again. He sprung out of bed, freshened up in the bathroom, and quickly changed into a new set of clothes straight out of a Bollywood movie.

They walked to the restaurant and sat down on plush pillows surrounding a low floor table. Guddu entered a moment later and took a seat on a pillow as well. He asked, "You had a good nap!" Even though it was a question, Guddu's bellowing voice often came out like a statement.

"I did, that felt great. And now I'm ready to grub! What are we having?"

"Here, we do not eat meat and we do not have any alcohol. The food is prepared fresh every day, is very healthy, and very delicious."

Food began to come out of the kitchen. The veggies were cooked, rich in color, and when he tore off a piece of roti and dipped it into one of the dishes, his mouth was filled with exotic spices and flavor.

"Man, this is good right here! Reminds me of the food my mom used to make growing up. My favorites were *aloo gobi* and *dal makhani,* so she would cook those dishes and leave them piping hot in the crockery so we could graze whenever we felt hungry. That was good stuff right there."

"You see, you are an Indian! Ah ah ah ah ah ah ah ah ah ah ah!!"

After enjoying dinner together, Guddu gave the final instructions for the night. "When you are finished, I have asked Nikki to take you to one of the yoga halls and work on the last two skills you need. We normally teach all of this to people over many weeks, but as you only have a few weeks, you are getting a full dose. You are very capable, though, and I can see you are absorbing everything. You are on a fast path.

"You learned lesson #2 before, which is to manage your energy. Tonight you will learn something most people don't know or don't believe is possible. With this skill, you will find its uses and applications in all areas of life. Not only in meditation. Tonight, you will learn how to **move energy**.

"As for me, I will be moving my energy to bed. Ah ah ah ah ah ah ah ah ah ah ah!!!"

INFUSE YOUR ENERGY

WITH A GOAL

And with that, Guddu got up, as did Nikki and A-Luv. Nikki touched Guddu's feet, and he put his hand on her head to bless her again. Without missing a beat, A-Luv got up and fell into Guddu's big embrace. Guddu left in one direction, and Nikki led A-Luv in the opposite direction. It was dark outside now and the grand Himalayas were in bed, no longer visible. Overhead in the dark blue sky, millions of stars shone down, glittering off the Ganges. The two walked up a short flight of stairs into a studio and took off their slippers. Surrounding the studio were candlelights reflecting off the mirrors, creating a warm dim glow. Nikki brought out two mats and placed them on the floor for them to sit on.

"I'm going to show you how to move your energy, and you've got to trust me. This is hard for most people at first, but I will get you there. Do you remember when we sat in the meditation garden and I asked you close to your eyes and move your awareness? I asked you to be aware of the warmth in your body. We're going to go there again, and then get deeper."

"Start by closing your eyes and visualizing how you are sitting on the floor. Sneak a peek at yourself in the mirror if you'd like, but then close your eyes again. Visualize your body." Nikki paused and let a minute pass by before continuing. "Now visualize that your body is filled with energy. It can help to imagine a transparent blue color filling up your body from your toes all the way up to your head. Visualize that energy running through all your nerves into every cell in your body. Now feel the warmth of this energy permeating your body. Feel that tingling sensation. Concentrate, and try to feel it in other areas of your body. See if you can heighten the sensation by being more aware of it. That heat you feel is the energy in your body, and the tingling is the energy moving throughout your body. Get familiar with this feeling so you can recognize it and call upon feeling it whenever you want. Now open your eyes. Were you able to feel the heat energy in your body?"

"I could feel a little something but I'm not sure if that was energy or just my imagination. It was pretty faint."

"Well done. That's really good that you could pick up even a hint of the energy. Let's focus our awareness on a single part of the body and see if you can pick up the heat energy there. Rub your palms together quickly like Mr. Miyagi, till you feel them get hot. Now separate your hands and put them an inch apart. Can you feel the heat transferring from your palms to your opposite palm? Try it again, warm up your palms and see if you can feel the energy."

"I can! I can feel that heat. Is that energy? It almost feels like something is between my hands. When I spread my hands apart then bring them back to an inch apart, it almost feels like an energy bubble is between my palms."

"That's it! You're doing great. That is your energy and you are absolutely feeling it. Know the energy in you is the same energy in me, and is the same energy in everything and everyone else. We are all connected by the same energy.

"Now let's move it.

"Hold up your hand and make a fist with only your pointer finger standing up. Focus all your awareness at the tip of your index finger. Hold it there and slowly move your gaze down the finger, crossing the first line, then the second line, until you reach the bottom line. Now bring your gaze back up just as slowly. Take your time, don't do this fast. When you start at the top and bring your focus down the finger, what does it feel like?"

"I don't know, I don't feel anything."

"Let's try it again. Start at the top and this time, imagine your finger is filled with that translucent blue energy. Bring your focus slowly down the finger. Did you feel anything this time?"

"It felt like the blue energy was draining out of it. I could picture the blue energy going down and I could pick up a light sensation of something actually leaving the finger. Was that it?"

"Yes, that is it. It's faint right now but that is exactly the feeling of moving energy. Start practicing with a finger and when you've got that, move on to two fingers till you've done the whole hand. When you can do the whole hand, you'll have enough of the skills needed for meditation. Inside of meditation, you'll be moving energy out of every limb and your torso, into your spine. When you gather energy in your spine, you feel centered."

They sat in silence as A-Luv continued practicing moving energy up and down one finger, then a second, until he was able to move it in all fingers of both hands. The sensation was a light tingling feeling that started at his fingertips and moved down to his wrist. As he moved it back up, the energy dispersed from the concentrated source at the wrist, through the palm, and flooding each finger.

STILLNESS
IS PEACE

"I got it. It's super faint still, but I can feel it. I know it'll get stronger with practice, but I get what we're looking for. This is crazy, I had no idea you could move energy in your body, but it makes sense."

"Now it's time for the last lesson: **life-force breathing**. When you control your breath, you experience benefits. The breath is the first thing you take in when you are born and the last thing when you die. Learning different breathing techniques can be like smoking indica—it'll lower your stress, blood pressure, anxiety, and depression while simultaneously increasing your energy levels and relaxing your muscles. We take breathing for granted because it's automatic, but when you learn these techniques, you'll get even more benefit out of each breath.

"Lie back and place your hand over your diaphragm. Now inhale through your nose and fill up your diaphragm, like you're filling your belly with breath. Your hand and belly will rise if you're doing it right. If you're filling up only your lungs, you're doing it wrong. I see you've got it. Good. Now breathe like this for three minutes."

After three minutes went by, Nikki said, "Shift your awareness to observe your state of mind. How has it changed from before and after you did the breathing exercise?"

"I definitely feel way more calm and don't have that jittery feeling that I often seem to live with. The best way I can describe it is I feel still inside."

"That's fantastic. That stillness is peace. Most people never experience calmness, as they live in a constant state of anxiety and stress. But imagine having that type of calm even during high pressure situations. Now I want to show you a second breathing technique. Go ahead and sit back up and this time, you're going to regulate your breath. When you inhale, breath in for five counts and then exhale for five counts. You're going to do this for three minutes now. Ready, begin."

At first, inhaling for five counts was pretty easy but oddly enough, A-Luv found that he was running out of breath to exhale around the fourth count. He had to literally push air out to get to the fifth count. Then he took a deep inhale since he was out of air and went too hard, so he struggled to pull in the last count and then when he exhaled, it all came shooting out of his nose. After a few rounds, he settled into a rhythm, and once he got it, he kept it.

"How did that feel?"

"Interesting. At first, I struggled to exhale, then I struggled to inhale. Overall, I didn't seem to have as much air to exhale as I was inhaling, which is weird."

"We tend to take more breaths than we need to," said Nikki. "That's because we have weak breathing muscles in our ribs called intercostals, and don't expunge all the air from our lungs. So we take a short breath in to compensate. Obviously, you can't breathe like this all the time, but starting off your meditation with breathing exercises helps oxygenate the body and bring you to an inner state of calm. It's also useful outside of meditation and literally why people say, 'take a deep breath' whenever someone gets mad."

"I don't know if this is true or not, but I remember reading it and thinking it was interesting. I read that humans take about twelve to twenty breaths a minute, whereas some species who breathe less live longer. Elephants take only four to five breaths a minute and when resting, alligators can take only one breath a minute. Dogs take forty to fifty breaths a minute. So maybe one way to live longer is to breathe slower. I'm down with cryogenics but this is way cheaper!"

They both laughed and then decided to call it a night. "Get some rest, my friend," Nikki said. "Tomorrow morning we're going to put it all together."

CREATE A MEDITATION RITUAL

The next morning, A-Luv joined Nikki in the yoga studio. They sat on chairs with hard backs and seat cushions. "It doesn't matter if you sit on the floor, in a chair, or in your car. What matters is that sitting for a long period of time doesn't create so much discomfort that you lose your concentration. Ideally, you'd want to create a morning ritual to meditate at the same time, the same place, and the same way every day. Early morning is best, so you have peace and quiet as you learn how to meditate. Do your best to protect that time. Think of it like having an appointment with yourself. Don't be so rigid that missing the morning causes you to forget about meditating the rest of the day. If you can't do the morning, find time at any other point in your day or even right before you sleep. What matters is that you get it in. As you develop a stronger meditation practice, you will be able to meditate in any environment. No checking your texts or emails either, mister. You want to have all your energy focused for this one moment. You ready to begin?

"Close your eyes and bring your awareness to your breath. Do diaphragmatic breathing for one minute. Breath deep into your belly. Feel the softness around your waist expand as you pull in air for five counts. Breathe out slowly, feel your belly and chest gently fall for five counts.

"Focus on the rhythm and the sensations of your breathing. The warmth of the air, the sensations in your nose, to the slight oceanic sound in the back of your throat.

"Now breathe in for five counts and out for five counts. Do that for a minute.

"Feel the warmth in your body. Visualize yourself seated and your nervous system filled with energy from your toes to your head.

SHIFT YOUR AWARENESS

"Next you're going to withdraw the energy from your left leg, starting at your toes. Focus your awareness at your toes and move your awareness up your foot, into your shin, to your knee, up into your thigh, through your hip, and into your spine. Feel the energy in your spine.

"Now do the same for your right leg. Start at your toes and move up your foot, into your shin, to your knee, up into your thigh, through your hip, and into your spine. Feel double the energy now in your spine.

"Next you're going to do this with your left arm. Start at the fingertips of your left hand and begin withdrawing the energy through your palm and wrist, into your forearm, through your elbow, into your upper arm and shoulder, through your torso, and into your spine.

"Now move your awareness to your right arm. Start at the fingertips of your right hand and begin withdrawing the energy through your palm and wrist, into your forearm, through your elbow, into your upper arm and shoulder, through your torso, and into your spine.

"Keep your energy stored in your spine and visualize your goal. See it and then feel it. Feel what it is like to achieve that quality in yourself or to accomplish that objective. Let that feeling run through your body and stay there for a while. Let that feeling seep in.

FEEL THE ENERGY IN YOUR SPINE

"Now infuse the energy in your spine with this feeling. Let that feeling flow down through the back of your neck and into your spine. The energy in your spine is now infused with this goal and it's time to move that energy through the rest of your body.

"This time going in reverse order, move energy out from your spine through the right side of your torso, up through your shoulder, into the upper arm and through the elbow, down into your forearm, wrist and palm, and finally into your fingertips.

"Do the same on your left side. Move energy out from your spine through the left side of your torso, up through your shoulder, into the upper arm and through the elbow, down into your forearm, wrist and palm, and finally into your fingertips.

"Now move energy from your spine through your right hip, down your right thigh, through your knee and into your shin, passing through your ankle, into your feet, and ending at the tips of your toes.

"Next move energy from your spine through your left hip, down your left thigh, through your knee and into your shin, passing through your ankle, into your feet, and ending at the tips of your toes.

"Your body is now filled with this newly infused energy. Shift your awareness to your newly uplifted inner vibes.

"Draw your awareness outwards and become aware of your body, feel your hands, feet, and head radiating with this energy.

"Slowly open your eyes and stay there for at least a minute, and bask in the glow of your meditation. Be aware of what you're feeling, absorb your vibrations into every cell of your body, then radiate your energy into the universe. You've completed your first meditation."

BASK IN
THE GLOW

OF YOUR
MEDITATION

As they left the yoga studio, A-Luv felt two things at once: super chill inside and crazy vibes pouring out of his skin. It reminded him of his first mushroom trip. The trip was so intense that he couldn't keep his eyes open, and it felt like some sort of energy was beaming out of every pore of his skin. He put on a jacket despite the hotel suite having a fireplace and the heater on, just so he could contain some of the energy pouring out of him. He stayed there for hours. While his eyes were closed and he was sitting still, he was conscious the whole time. It was like being aware of being in a dream but having no bodily sensation at all.

A-Luv enjoyed feeling present and aware of all his sensations at once. 'Shrooms opened the door to creativity and flow like he had never experienced. Drugs allowed A-Luv to instantly lower his inhibition and increase his sensitivity so his mind was bombarded with new information and feelings, and lyrics just poured out of him. He had no control of his awareness during his trips, so his mind would wander to all the new intense sensations including the bad emotions and thoughts. More than once, A-Luv self-induced a bad trip, spiraling him into fear, anxiety, and self-hate.

He turned to other drugs to self-induce his creative flow. A deep sense of insecurity, and lack of control and awareness coupled with the pressure to spit flows caused

A-Luv to fall into an addiction that almost killed him. Without his family and rehab, A-Luv had been on a path to self-destruction. Though he got clean, every day his awareness would wander back to using drugs. Every day was a test of willpower not to relapse.

While he was meditating, he experienced a mild feeling that reminded him of his drug-induced trips. He felt the energy pouring through his skin, and closing his eyes intensified the sensation. It felt good. And then a thought occurred to him: what if 'shrooms and other hallucinogens are simply reducing inhibition and increasing sensitivity to the point where you experience presence in all its power? Is that not the same thing that's happening inside of meditation?

Maybe meditation could give A-Luv the same creative boost he always craved. Though meditation and drugs were clearly not the same thing, the effects of meditation were similar, while being slightly different. A-Luv's meditation gave him a controlled release of his inhibitions as he fell into a deeply relaxed state. He slowly became more sensitive to his senses and had the ability to control his awareness. Thus, he could easily control how he chose to process new sensations and information, especially the bad emotions and thoughts that constantly popped up in his mind. He no longer attached his awareness to the negative, and as a result did not have a bad trip during his meditation. He was strengthening the positive thoughts and feelings by choosing to allocate more energy and awareness to them. He didn't feel overstimulated; he felt alive with more energy and clarity than ever, without the drugs.

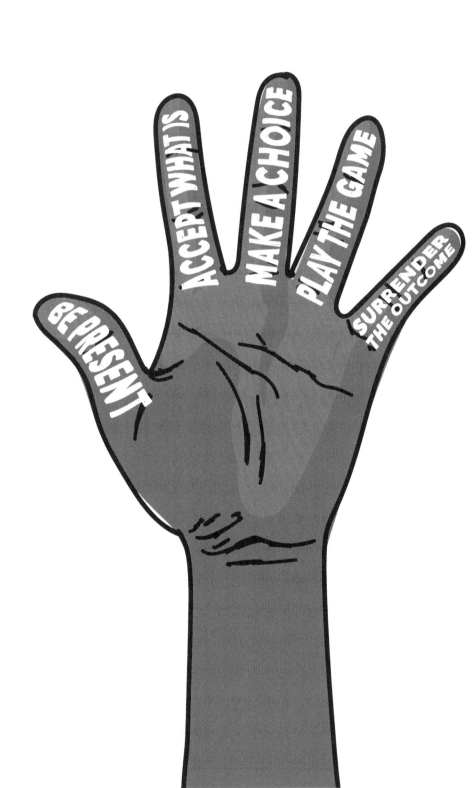

5

FIVE FINGERS

Nikki and A-Luv walked in silence toward the restaurant for breakfast. Guddu's booming voice met them. "Good morning!! How was your meditation?"

"Good morning, Guddu!" A-Luv said with a surprisingly upbeat vibe, given that he felt so chill coming out of meditation. "I don't even have the words for it. It was intense, beautiful, calming...I don't know how to describe it, but I feel amazing. And I'm grateful to have such an incredible teacher in Nikki."

"You're too sweet. I learned from the master himself. I'm simply a channel for his teaching. You are the one who is learning and applying it so quickly. It's quite impressive to see the speed of your growth."

Guddu had a surprise for A-Luv. "Today, we are going

to go white water rafting on Gangaji. You will meet one of the finest people there, who runs our operation. So let us finish up breakfast, put on your shorts, and we shall head down."

"Nikki, you coming with us?" A-Luv asked, hopeful to have her company.

"I would love to, but I have many things to do here as we have so many guests and I still need to prepare for the summit, as it's right around the corner. Go have fun, and I'll see you when you get back."

On their drive to the put-in location, A-Luv took the opportunity to learn more about Guddu's businesses, because he still couldn't understand how it all came to fruition. Guddu was never one to take credit for his achievements, and he didn't talk about business, either. A-Luv saw himself not only as a successful artist but as an entrepreneur, too. The first business he started was a record label to give him the artistic freedom and the cheddar. He called it *Flow*, a term used to describe the way rappers lay down lyrics over a beat. Flow was also the feeling when he was in the zone, and the progression of his life. A triple entendre.

As he started to sign other acts to the label, he realized that they too needed to market themselves to help them sell more records, so he started a marketing agency under the *Flow* banner. He found that more than just his artists were signing up for their services. He tried some ideas that didn't pan out, like a streaming service that paid the artists more royalties, but he later realized it didn't work, because his intention was to make more money, not to deliver something unique to listeners.

Seeing how Guddu went from runaway to runaway success, he wanted to better understand Guddu's approach and absorb whatever he could to continue building his businesses. Guddu resumed his explanation when they stopped for chai in the restaurant of his hotel overlooking Laxman Jhula.

**SUFFERING
IS A CHOICE**

"I told you how the idea for the hotel came about. I did not set out to build a hotel; I had very little interest. But guests kept coming from all over the world, and they could not all stay with me. One day, the property next to my shop came for sale, and I thought that would be a fine place to build a hotel. Our guests could have a comfortable place to stay, a beautiful view, great food, access to all the yoga and meditation centers, and they could easily come to my shop if they wished. My wife said she would like to run it and thank goodness, she is not lazy like me! Ah ah ah ah ah ah ah ah ah!!

"Immediately after building the hotel, we again were out of room for all our guests. All these wonderful people on spiritual journeys would come here to take yoga and meditation courses. More and more of these little shops opened up along this road, but when I looked at them, I thought they were very dingy. I would never go there myself, but people kept coming back. Many dishonest people saw that they could make a healthy living off these foreigners, but they were not actually helping them find inner peace and calm. I knew because thousands of people came to my shop and would open up to me about their suffering. I could see their pain, like I saw yours, and I wanted to help them in an honest way. I never worried about making money. I knew that once I had the inspiration or calling to create a safe haven for these spiritual travelers, my job was simply to make it the best it could be.

I did not worry whether money would come or not. But how could it not, when the universe has already provided me with so much?"

A-Luv had never heard someone so humble, taking no credit, and accomplishing so much without stress or pain in the process. He realized that he had a false belief: in order for something to be worth it, he had to suffer to get it. Isn't that the core philosophy of the American Dream? That if you sacrificed your life, you could become rich. How bass-ackwards was that? Guddu showed him a universal truth, a truth so powerful that it shook him to his core: **suffering is a choice.**

YOU DON'T HAVE TO SUFFER

TO GET WHAT YOU WANT

They pulled into a long dirt road that declined toward the river and came to a stop when they reached a building. As they got out of the car, a tall Indian man walked out with the biggest, brightest, whitest smile you've ever seen. He didn't slow his pace as he approached Guddu and walked full force into a giant embrace. The two squeezed each other tightly and you could sense the exchange of love and energy through their embrace. "Guddu!! Welcome, how are you, my brother?!" exclaimed Arjun in an American accent.

"You must be A-Luv, what up my man?!" The two fluidly went in for a mid-five, pulled each other in, swung one arm around the other's back, and gave each other an open-palm slap on the back while keeping their hands interlocked. They bro hugged.

"What's up, bro? What's your name?"

"My name's Arjun, but you can call me AI."

"Oh snap, like Allen Iverson. You from Philly?"

"In...West Philadelphia..."

"Born and raised," the two of them rapped in unison.

"Haha!!! That's what's up!" said A-Luv as they gave each other dap.

"I can tell you boys will get along just fine. AI used to be called Dr. I in his past life. He has a very interesting story— make sure you ask him about it when you're in the raft together."

A-Luv liked AI immediately. He had such a positive vibe and he liked code-switching back into street slang.

They went through the safety briefing, put on helmets and a life vest, and packed a dry bag with their afternoon lunch and a warm layer of clothing in case it got cold. A-Luv and AI put-in first, and Guddu's raft trailed directly behind them.

"Have you ever been rafting before or is this your first time?" asked AI.

"I've been before, but never in a two-man raft and definitely not through real rapids."

"Ah man, this is gonna be epic! We've got a lot of time on the river together, which is perfect. While we're out here having a good time, I'm going to share with you what I call the Five Fingers of Life."

"Oh! Sorta like Sway's Five Fingers of Death?"

"Exactly! I saw you freestyle on Sway's show—that was fire!"

"Yeah man, that was fun. When I get into my zone, the lyrics come off the dome."

BE PRESENT

A-Luv had one of the most legendary appearances on Sway's Five Fingers of Death, a freestyle challenge where rappers are given five different beats and each beat gets progressively harder. The rapper doesn't know what instrumental is coming and has to switch up their flows and lyrics without missing a beat. The biggest challenge for MCs is to be completely present. The minute they think, they freeze. For those who get through all five beats, Sway crowns them "real MCs" and challenges all other rappers to freestyle on his show. A-Luv was only one of three rappers to accept Sway's additional hurdle, the random word generator, where Sway threw out a random word every few bars and A-Luv rapped about it.

"Well, that flow state you get when freestyling is the same zone I get when I hit a rapid. It's also the first finger of life: **be present.** One of the reasons I love rafting, and why people love extreme sports, is that it forces you to be present, to be right here in the now. You get this intense rush of being alive that is free from all problems, time, thinking, and personality. If you slip away from the present during a dangerous moment, it can literally mean death. Unfortunately, people depend on that high-risk activity to get into that intense state of presence, but they can access that state now. We've got a rapid coming up, so I want you to concentrate on paddling forward through the rapid. Don't think about anything else. Be present. Here we go!"

Their raft approached a class III rapid with A-Luv paddling forward and AI keeping the raft pointed straight. When they hit the rapid, it bumped A-Luv, but he had his foot wedged into the raft and kept his balance, all the while continuing to paddle. Water splashed as the raft rocked up and down, soaking them in the process. They made it safely through the rapid. "Wooooooooooo!" A-Luv yelled. "That was *dope!*" The river was calm again. They turned around to watch Guddu and his guide safely navigate the rapids as well.

"Bro, that was intense! I almost went swimming, but my foot held on tight. What a rush!"

"You did great! We're about to come up on a class IV rapid though, so get ready."

A-Luv was still reeling in the rush of the last rapid and didn't realize how fast they came up to the next rapid. AI yelled, "paddle, paddle," but by that time it was too late. Their raft headed straight for a massive rock that had water gushing over it and into an abyss.

As soon as A-Luv looked up, *wham*, the boat capsized. A-Luv was pinned underneath the raft in the icy Himalayan water, tossed in a torrent as if he was in a washer's spin cycle.

What in the…! What's happening?? Ok, the raft pinned me under, and I'm getting tossed around in the water, and all I have is the one breath! Please don't let me die, I don't wanna drown. I'm not going to drown. Ok, move your arms and try to get some air but don't panic. You have to get out from under this raft or else you're not going to make it. Move fast, go go!

He scrambled his hands and made it out from under the raft with his head still underwater. He felt a hand on his shoulder, AI pulling A-Luv's head up out of the water.

Gasp!! Whoa that was close. Whoa that was close.

AI was on top of the capsized raft, holding on to A-Luv who struggled to stay afloat. The river hauled the raft through the rapids. The water's forced dragged A-Luv into rocks, almost breaking his grip with AI.

In a brief moment, the river jammed the boat onto a rock and AI desperately tried to pull A-Luv up to safety, but A-Luv was too heavy. In the next instant, a gush of water dislodged the raft, forcing it toward more rapids.

The raft violently hit another rock. A-Luv scrambled to find footing on the rock. Just as the raft was heaved away by the current, A-Luv found a foothold and propelled himself onto the raft.

A-Luv and AI were gasping for breath on all fours when they heard Guddu's voice, "Get left, get left! There are more rapids ahead. It's not over yet."

A-Luv saw AI shake his head in dismay.

"AI, we gotta go."

Both quickly jumped back in the water, pulling the raft against the current toward the left side of the river. Grinding, running, and digging deep as hard as they could, they made it to the bank. Guddu and his guide came over, flipped the raft right-side up, and dropped the anchor.

Both men quickly removed their icy clothes to avoid getting hypothermia. They still had five hours to float down the river. A-Luv remembered seeing Bear Grylls in a *Man Versus Wild* episode saying, "If you ever get hypothermic, start doing pushups." So A-Luv took off his clothes and started knocking out pushups to get some blood in his body.

Their dry bag had dumped out of the boat, along with A-Luv's paddle. Guddu and his guide pulled warm clothes from their dry bag for A-Luv and AI to wear. They all rested for ten minutes and decided to get back in, because they still had another couple hours before reaching their campsite for lunch, and five hours downriver before reaching the van that would bring them back to the top where they began.

As A-Luv and AI got up, they embraced and felt so grateful they had survived.

ACCEPT

AND MOVE ON

They found A-Luv's paddle caught in some plant growth on the side of the river, a relief for the journey ahead. They floated the next two hours in silence. Both men were simply present and felt so happy to be alive after their near-death experience. When the campsite approached, they paddled to the right and took out the raft. Guddu and his guide did the same and the second his feet touched the sand, Guddu declared, "So...now you can tell all your friends back home that you've done naked pushups on the side of an Indian river! Ah ah ah ah ah ah ah ah ah ah!!"

That broke the silence. Like all good adventures, half the fun is in retelling the story. Each man went around sharing his experience both from the perspective of being in the flipped raft and the perspective of seeing it flip while running the rapids. Guddu took the opportunity to share some wisdom. "Whenever you experience any situation, let it pass right through you. Do not let the energy get stuck or else it is ten times more difficult to release it. Just like water passes over rocks, let this pass. That does not mean to be foolish, but we can all be happy to be alive without suffering through that story over and over again. Accept and move on."

When they got back in their rafts and pushed back out to the river, A-Luv asked AI what Guddu meant by "accept and move on." "That's actually the second finger of life: **accept and move on.** What Guddu means is: don't create resistance with life, just accept what is because there's no other option. Wishing something were different doesn't change it. Accepting is not the same as agreeing. He taught me that we don't need to agree in order to accept. It's when we don't fully accept someone or something that we create our own suffering. Resistance equals suffering."

RESISTANCE

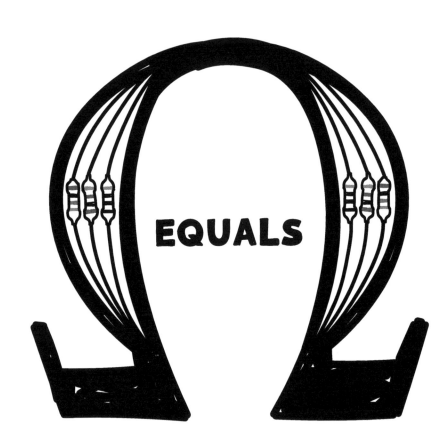

EQUALS

SUFFERING

All this made sense to A-Luv in theory, but he wanted an example to make sure what he thought he understood was internalized as the right lesson. "Do you have an example of something you accepted rather than resisted? How did it play out?"

"For sure. When I first met Guddu and learned to meditate, he sent me to Vashishta Cave which is an ancient cave with incredible vibes, perfect for meditation. I walked inside and found a place to sit next to a small shrine. My eyes closed and went into a deep meditative state for the next hour and a half.

"Till suddenly...I felt a knock on my knee and ice-cold water all over my lap! I opened my eyes and saw the Punditji standing beside me, and he said, '*Koi baat nahi, beta. Ganga ka pani hai.*' (Don't worry, son. It's water from the Ganges.)

"His bucket of holy water bumped my knee, tipping it over on my lap. I just started to laugh. I guess the universe thought, 'Meditation over, time to go!' I dried off by sunning on a rock on the banks of Gangaji and thought to myself, 'what a gift.' You see how much fun you can have if you accept and laugh instead of resist and get mad?"

AI's story hit A-Luv like a ton of bricks. How many life situations and people had he not fully accepted and, as a result, got hot and bothered?

He would say things like "this shouldn't be this way," "he should be like this," "no one ought to feel that way," or "I shouldn't have to deal with this." And there were plenty of times where he'd spin a story around the facts of a situation and end up being judgmental.

He now realized he could have accepted those situations without having to suffer as a result: "This *is* this way," "he *is* like this," "they *do* feel that way," and "I *am* dealing with this."

AI explained the simple act of acceptance prevents energy from getting stuck and prevents attracting more negative energy like a magnet. "Bad vibes are incredibly strong in attracting your soul. Next thing you know, you've lost yourself. And when you stop being objective, you end up saying or doing something you regret or that didn't lead to the best outcome."

"You know how much energy I've wasted on resisting what is?" lamented A-Luv. "And you know what, none of it mattered. I still had to deal with whatever was in front of me. Wishing it was different didn't do me a lick of good."

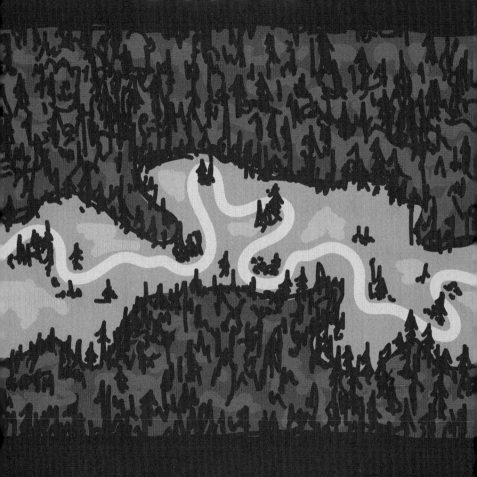

FIND THE PATH

OF LEAST RESISTANCE

They continued floating down the river. A-Luv watched the water find the path of least resistance, constantly moving and always flowing. Water doesn't seek balance, it finds equilibrium based on whatever life brings its way. If A-Luv had not accepted that he had been tossed from the raft, pinned under the water with only one breath, he would have died. If he started thinking "this isn't fair," or "why me," or any other variation of resistance, he would have run out of air. His instantaneous acceptance saved his life.

"So after you accept, what comes next?" asked A-Luv, ready to keep the teachings coming.

"My man, I love it! Before I talk about that, take a look ahead and let me know if you see which way the water is flowing more smoothly around that rock. To the left or to the right?"

A-Luv stood up at the bow of the raft, careful not to lose his balance, and saw what appeared to be a class II or III rapid ahead. Nonetheless, he wasn't going to underestimate it. The water appeared to turn white on the right side of the rock, so he signaled to AI that they should go left. He sat down and began to paddle forward while AI paddled and steered them to the left of the rock in smooth water.

"Nice work! That was definitely the right choice. So where were we? Oh right, you asked me what comes after acceptance. Well we just did it: **choose what's next**. That's the third finger of life. When you've accepted the fact that there's a rock ahead and it's creating rapids with whitewater, you simply evaluate your options based on reality and choose what's next. What you didn't say was "let's go back" or "let's go get an engine to motor through it."

"Ha! That's pretty easy, then."

"It is pretty easy, but that comes with practice. Choices often have trade-offs and aren't as simple as deciding between smooth and rough water. More often, you're faced with options that don't feel perfectly right, because you'll receive conflicting messages from others and worse, yourself. Well, from your ego, more precisely. The more awake your soul is, the more that one voice will get stronger and decisions will be easier to make. In the meantime, while your ego's voice is articulate and loud, it will give you advice to please itself. And even worse, it can be a wolf disguised in sheep's clothing. Sometimes your ego plays dress up in words like status, prestige, and legacy. Guddu taught me a line that helped me navigate those tough choices until my soul could speak for itself: "Am I doing the right things, with the right people, for the right reasons?"

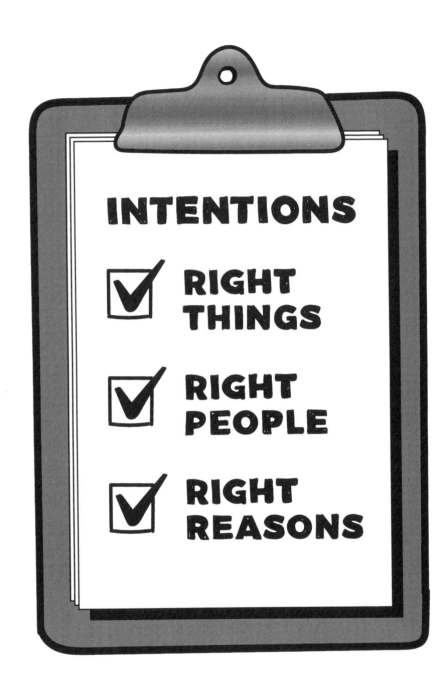

Am I doing the right things, with the right people, for the right reasons? I feel like the answer is mostly yes, but let's see for real. My last relationship was definitely with the wrong person, but I ended that. But it did take me a while. Did I know she was the wrong person and still stay with her? I did. Why did I? What's something I agonized over recently? Oh I know, it was buying my house. Part of me was saying I didn't need a house that big all to myself. The other part of me was saying you have the money, enjoy. But if I'm honest, I bought it because it would let people know I made it. And yeah, I love the beach, but I needed them to admire me and my crib. So, was I doing the right thing in buying a house? Yeah. With the right people? Yeah. For the right reasons? No, I can honestly tell myself that. I could have still bought it but without feeding my ego.

AI spotted some people at a campsite playing beach volleyball and hollered to A-Luv and Guddu, "Ayo! You guys wanna go play some volleyball and then take a dip in the water after?" A-Luv recognized the campsite from his drive upriver to the yoga retreat center.

"Yes! That looks fun, let's go" returned Guddu. This man was always up for an adventure.

They maneuvered their rafts to the shore and got out. "Hey, everyone! Any chance we can join you for a game?" asked AI. His enthusiasm and infectious energy seemed to always get a "yes" out of life, and this was no exception.

The campers were happy to greet their new guests and turn their game into a 4v4 match.

AI made a great blocker and spiker upfront. A-Luv's PE classes from back in LA panned out for him, he served and dug pretty well. Guddu's guide could hit the ball up and back over, and Guddu was everywhere; serving, digging, spiking, and setting. After a couple matches, they thanked their hosts and sat on the sand with their feet in the water to relax.

"Wow, Guddu. You sure can move for an old man!"

PLAY THE GAME OF LIFE

"Ah ah ah ah ah ah ah ah ah ah ah ah!!! Well if you are going to play the game, then play the game. This is the fourth finger of life: **play the game**. I see how much fun kids have playing, and somehow when we get older, we want to stop playing and we want to manage the team. Then we want to own the team. Then we lose interest. That's because we stopped playing! Leave managerial and ownership duties to others. You are an A-player or else your name wouldn't be A-Luv. Ah ah ah ah ah ah ah ah ah ah ah ah!!

"A-players don't sit out and watch. Too many people want to control and not play the game of life. Life is *lila*, or game, as we say. There can only be one lion in the jungle. Be the lion!"

"Heck yeah, I'm down with that! I still love writing and going into the studio, but I just don't do it enough anymore. I feel like my attention is pulled in so many different directions."

"That is of your own design. Accept that fact and now decide what to do. And once you decide, go all out. Don't hold back. Your mind is an incredible tool for this, so use it. Apply your brain at this point and give your idea form. Visualize what you will do, see it, and then feel it. Once you have that clarity, go play and enjoy!"

Guddu sprung up, put on his life vest and helmet, and

jumped into the flowing river! His guide grabbed the raft and A-Luv looked at AI in shock. "Is he crazy?!"

"Haha! This area of the river is called 'water slide.' It's totally safe for you to go in and ride the small rapids. Just put on your helmet and life vest, and I'll pick you up in the raft." A-Luv didn't once think about the near-death experience he had just gone through. The energy wasn't stuck. He jumped up, put on his gear and dove in! The high-water flow in this area made for a fun and easy ride, just as its name suggested. A-Luv pointed his feet down-river and held onto the sides of his life vest. As he ripped and rumbled through the rapids, he felt exhilarated.

Guddu's guide pulled up beside Guddu and pulled him into the raft. AI did the same for A-Luv. A-Luv observed the energy in his body coursing through his nervous system after getting shocked by the cold water and now basking in the sun. He felt totally present and stoked that he had put his newly learned skill of awareness into real-life.

"Bro, I wish I could do this every day. Now I get why you run this rafting business! Is that why you left being a doc?"

"Ah man, I'm not even gonna front like I had this all planned out. But I sure am glad things panned out how they did."

"You gotta tell me the story. What happened?" A-Luv asked as he wrung water from his shorts.

SURRENDER

THE
OUTCOME

"I've got to give credit to Guddu. He showed me the fifth and final finger of life: **surrender the outcome**. When I say surrender, I don't mean give up. I mean don't get attached to the outcome. Guddu has never cared what happens. He lives a very uncomplicated life as a result, and you can see the joy it brings. I wanted this type of joy too, and when I met Guddu I was faced with one of the biggest decisions in my life: whether or not to sell my practice.

"I was an orthodontist and my practice had several locations in Colorado and southern California. We grew every year and even though I'm young, I got offers to buy my practice all the time. I never seriously considered it until a deal came to me that made me consider it. They say great businesses aren't sold they're bought. Well they were trying to buy me. It was a pure cash grab and would have purely been for the money. But we're talking a lot of money.

"While I was entertaining the idea and eventual offer, I also noticed something happening in our industry. These corporations were buying up practices like mine to roll up the industry. The same thing happened in dentistry. I saw how the quality of patient care was dropping because more cases were coming to me to fix poorly done work. I saw how many unnecessary procedures were being done to drive up profit. And I saw how the quality of life for the orthodontist worsened as they traded having their own practice and setting their own schedules for a payday. I had a choice: either sell to one of these corporations or not.

"I had planned a trip to India during this time and a friend of mine had just gotten back. He suggested I meet this amazing man named Guddu. I figured I'd stop in since I was already going to be nearby. When I met with Guddu, he could see that I was struggling. He asked me why and when I told him the decision I struggled with, he said, 'You already know the answer.'

"He was right—I did know the answer, but I couldn't rationalize it with my mind. My mind was saying you're in the business of making money and this will make you lots of money. But I didn't feel right about it, and I confessed as much to Guddu. Guddu's response to me was, 'Your choices are to do something for your ego or your soul. Your ego wants to do it for money and notoriety. Your soul wants to help patients and doctors. The only reason this is an issue for you is because you have not surrendered the outcome. When you are not attached to the outcome of making money, and focus instead on doing what is right for you, then the decision is easy. All your life since the day you were born, the universe has provided for you. What are you so worried about? You will still be provided for but perhaps in a way you didn't expect. The choice is easy.'"

"So I'm guessing you didn't sell. But then how did you end up here?"

ACCEPT WHAT LIFE PRESENTS

"You're right, I didn't sell. And when I sent a letter to the acquiring firm, I felt a massive sense of relief. I listened to my soul and acted from there. I had completely surrendered the outcome, and figured life will show me what's next. The very next week, I got a call from an ortho buddy. There was a doctor-led group forming and my friend asked if I'd be interested in joining them. When I looked at the opportunity, I couldn't believe what I saw. This group of doctors was helping to improve patient care and make the lives of doctors even better. And, the opportunity was just as large as the one I had just turned down. The thing is, had I accepted the last deal, I would have been working for that company and would not have been allowed to get involved in this new opportunity due to a non-compete clause. Here was life, taking responsibility for me. I worked my tail off, don't get me wrong, but I didn't have to do it by hook or crook, as Guddu says.

"I returned on a trip to India not long after selling that company, and spent some time with Guddu. He shared with me how all these people were coming to the yoga retreat center and they sometimes wanted to take a break and do something off-campus. The inspiration came to me after I had spent a summer as a white water rafting guide. Here was this gorgeous river and no rafting companies. So Guddu and I formed a partnership because we enjoyed the idea of playing the game together. Now, I run this for a few months out of the year when the weather is good, and then I return to the US the rest of the year during off-season. Life has been good to me, and I let it."

"Bro, I have so many questions! First of all, that's an incredible story. I don't feel like my life resembles that, and if I had surrendered, I don't think I'd be where I am today. Don't you feel like you could have sold to that company and changed it from the inside?"

"I might have been able to, but that wasn't my intention of selling to them. Had my intention been to get access and change their minds to provide better care for patients and doctors, then that would have been the right move for me. But that wasn't my intention, and I needed to be honest with myself. You see, two people can arrive at the same decision with two different intentions. My intention was to help patients and doctors, and I didn't feel I could make that happen inside that company."

"But don't you feel like all these things happen because you hustle? I feel like I've worked my tail off to get where I am and if I had just surrendered, I might not have achieved as much."

"I definitely hustle. But here's the thing, a lot of people work hard all their lives and don't get rewarded materially like we have. And others who have very little material success have peace and joy in their lives. So hustling doesn't have anything to do with happiness. You're gonna hustle no matter what anyways. You're not going to wake up one day and decide not to grind. That's who you are. The problem comes when you think that your hustle is what achieved the results. That's your ego tricking you. Your hustle contributed, but it's not the only reason."

"True that, there's definitely some higher power at play."

"But do you actually believe that? I ask because most people say, 'I only focus on what I can control.' The only thing we can control are our (A) thoughts, (B) emotions, and (C) actions. So even though we say we don't control the outcome, we expect life to look like this:

$$A + B + C = X$$

"The truth is much bigger than that. While we control those three variables, we don't control three others: (D) microeconomics, (E) macroeconomics, and (F) universal influences. So when I say we don't control the outcome, I literally mean that:

$$(A + B + C) + (D + E + F) = X$$

"When you realize this, it's much easier to surrender the outcome and focus on crushing the three variables within your control."

There was something about math and logic that always felt right to A-Luv. He remembered when he was learning addition and subtraction, his dad had asked him a word problem where he had to solve the age of person B where person A was 5 years old and person B was 2 years older. He knew how to count up and down, and how to add 5 + 2, but he couldn't solve the problem correctly. His dad figured out that A-Luv didn't know that *older* meant *add* and *younger* meant *subtract*. When he understood the language, he could solve the problem.

For the first time, A-Luv had been shown what it meant to not control all the variables. A simple math equation with a profound impact.

"I get it. It just clicked," he said to AI.

"Well done. For many people, they feel like they need to surrender to a higher power through faith. Call it life, the universe, God, whatever word doesn't block your energy from understanding the truth. And that's great for some people, whereas for others, they want a more scientific explanation. That's the beauty of the high vibe path— we're simply understanding energy at a much deeper level and realizing deeper truths within us. At some point, you're either going to feel it or you're not, and that feeling is what we're after."

Their destination was visible ahead, and their driver standing on the sand waiting for their arrival. They pulled up their rafts, loaded them onto the van, and headed back to the rafting office where their car was parked. Guddu checked in with A-Luv and asked, "Tell me, what did you understand about the Five Fingers of Life? I trust that AI guided you more than in the raft!"

He sure had. A-Luv took a breath before speaking, to center himself, and then he shared what he learned. "Well, aside from saving my life, he helped me realize what it actually means to live. The Five Fingers of Life make so much sense to me."

He held up his hand and used his fingers to count each lesson. "First, I've got to be present without my mind constantly chattering about the past or the future. There is only now. By harnessing my awareness and quieting my thoughts, I can experience the rush of being present like the rush of roaring down a rapid. Hopefully without falling out!

"Second, I simply need to accept what life is presenting and not create stories or judgment. By observing what is without attaching additional meaning to it, I can see the objects. That's not just external observation, that's also internal. Emotions and thoughts are objects too, and by observing and accepting those without creating stories around them, I can easily move to the next step.

"Third, I need to consider what options are actually in front of me and make a choice. Every decision aligned with my soul is the right one, and all I have to do is ask myself, 'Are you doing the right things, with the right people, for the right reasons?'

"Fourth, I've got to play the game. Once I've decided what I'm going to do, now it's time for me to go all in. I've got to use my mind to give the idea form. That means bringing all my resources and talents to bear to play the game of life. No need to be a spectator or up in the owner's box. The universe is actually the owner, but I'm the star player, so I need to hit that field and give it my all.

"Or in business terms, I realize that I'm not the CEO, I'm the COO. Life is the CEO and will unfold however it's going to, with or without my input. It has long before my existence and will long after it. My job is to get the orders and then execute.

"Fifth and finally, I need to surrender and let go of the outcome. Whatever happens is what was going to happen anyhow, so my job is to turn over the variables I don't control and focus on what I do.

"By following these five points, I am truly alive."

"Very good, very good! You have understood these lessons very well. I can see the shift in your consciousness happening. *Wah, kya baat hai.*"

He didn't merely repeat the words AI had said, he had internalized the meaning and used his intelligence to give it form for how it would look in his life. Guddu had been around long enough to know the difference between someone who says the words and someone who takes action. There was nothing lost in translation, even though the message was passed from person to person. The telephone game effect didn't occur, because they were speaking of universal truths. Words can be twisted and distorted, but truth is truth.

They arrived at the office building. AI and Guddu gave each other a huge hug. A-Luv felt sad. He had bonded so much with AI, and he didn't want to leave. AI walked up to him and put both hands on A-Luv's shoulders when he spoke. "My brother, it was an honor. I can't wait for our paths to cross again, and know that I'm just a Face-Time away if you want to rap out. I will always carry your energy with me, and know that you carry mine in you. We're never apart. One love."

Water started to well up in A-Luv's eyes. Normally he would hide it but now, he observed the emotion and accepted it. The deeper truth is that they were both vibing at a similar frequency, so their connection was strong, and that overwhelmed A-Luv with joy. He hugged AI goodbye and knew one thing: AI was a soul brother. "Brother, I can't thank you enough. You are a blessing in my life and if you're ever in my neck of the woods, hit me up. You got a backstage pass to my life. One love."

Guddu and A-Luv got into the SUV and Guddu said to the driver, *chalo use ek baar school dikhaate hain*. The car started to move. A-Luv rolled down his window and waved goodbye to AI who stood there waving until he was out of sight.

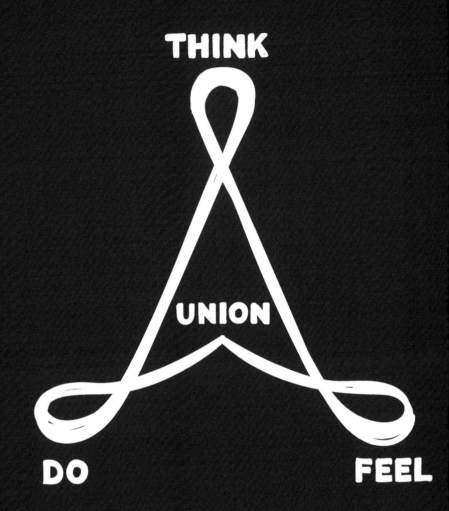

6

UNION

They pulled out of the yoga retreat center and drove along on the high mountain road with a view of the Ganges below. Several minutes passed in silence as A-Luv reflected on his near-death experience when Guddu finally broke the silence. "*Beta,* you are learning so well. But there is one thing you must know which I have not yet taught you. All of the blessings you have in life are not only for you. You must share them with others. See, look there at Gangama which is constantly in flow. Her fresh water is abundant and can be used for drinking, bathing, praying, so many things. Whereas still water cannot be used. It becomes dirty and filled with disease. There must be a flow of your material blessings that come to you too. You must not hoard it all for yourself or else it will create disease within yourself and with your relationships. As it comes, it must flow to help others."

For a long time now, A-Luv had been thinking about what he could do to help others. He already donated money to causes and did a charity concert here and there, but he felt like there was so much more to do. He didn't really know what that would be, and he worried about taking time away from making money. He didn't want to fade to black and become a has-been.

As he pondered, his awareness shifted from thinker to observer. He started to see the stories he told himself. The story that he didn't know what to do. The story that he wouldn't have enough money. The story that he didn't want to be forgotten. He looked down at his hand and counted it out. *My awareness is fully here and I'm observing these stories. Kill these stories and all that's left is the fact that I'm doing nothing now. I do have a platform through hip-hop and business resources I can deploy. My choices are simple: do nothing or do something. I choose to do something, but what? I don't know yet, but I will put my mind to it now that I feel called. And I'll give it my all without worrying about whether I've helped one person or a million.*

Less than a minute had passed, and he had arrived at his truth. No agonizing, no guilt or shame, and no ego holding him back. He was free.

SHARE LIFE'S BLESSINGS

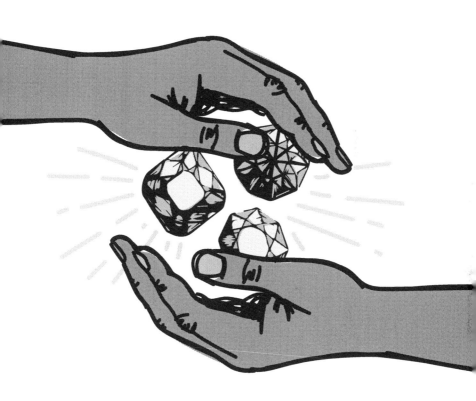

WITH OTHERS

The driver pulled up to a school and stopped the car. Guddu picked up his signature man-bag, a black bag containing a notebook and cash, and slung the thin strap around his neck. They were greeted by a woman who looked like a female version of Guddu, and A-Luv immediately sensed her vibe was just like Guddu's. The second they saw each other they hugged and both began laughing hysterically.

"Ah ah ah ah ah ah ah ah ah ah ah ah ah!!!"

"Ha ha ha ha ha ha ha ha ha ha ha ha ha!!!"

This easily went on for thirty seconds without a word being said. Finally, Guddu turned to A-Luv. "Come, meet my sister Nina."

A-Luv walked toward her and without a thought, bent down to touch her feet with his hands. Nina put her hand on top of his head and blessed him saying *kush raho* and then roared, "*Areey waah, Guddu! Tumne unko pair chhoona sikhaaya.* Bless you my son, what a beautiful thing you have learned here. *Chalo*, let's sit down and have some chai!"

This really was Guddu's sister. They sat down for chai and Nina said, "I believe you know my son, Rohan. He has told me about you for many years. It's nice to finally meet you."

"No way, your son is Rohan? I had no idea. I mean, I knew he was Guddu's nephew, but I hadn't put the connection together. Now it all makes sense. It's nice to meet you as well, Auntie."

Rohan talked about his family all the time, but A-Luv could never really tell who was blood family, close friends, or acquaintances, because Indians always called people their brothers, sisters, aunts, and uncles, even if they weren't. As a sign of respect, the younger generation doesn't call elders by their first name.

"When my sister retired, she decided to move back to India with her husband," Guddu explained. "I told her I wanted to start a school to help the kids growing up in poverty here in the Himalayas, and she loved the idea. She had been in the medical profession in the US and was a biology teacher in India before moving to the US. It was in fact her idea to build this garden here. Come take a look." They walked out of the entrance door to the side of the building, and there was a flourishing garden filled with fruits, vegetables, herbs, and of course, chili peppers.

"The garden serves many purposes for us here," Nina said. "First, the kids receive all their meals here. They are 100 percent vegetarian. Not all the food is grown here at the school, but we plant as much as we can and use every bit of what we harvest. The rest of the food comes from local farmers, many of whose kids either attend school here or have in the past. We do not charge tuition, so the school is free for all to attend. Second, we created a project-based curriculum to focus on teaching the whole student and the whole community, living the high vibe lifestyle. And third, the students do service projects such as planting this garden and helping others in the community, as a way to teach them practical skills and give them the theory behind it, all while doing something for the greater good."

"No way, this is unreal. So when you say you teach the high vibe lifestyle, does that mean you're teaching them what I've been learning?" asked A-Luv.

"Yes, that's exactly it," replied Nina. "You see, the word *yoga* means union. All is one. The poses you're familiar with are actually called *asanas*. So when we are teaching the whole student, we are teaching them just as much about themselves and their inner being as we are about the world and practical skills. Every student has a zero-period option where they can come here to meditate, or they can meditate at home. And we offer meditation as an after-school program as well. Instead of punishments when a child is misbehaving, we send them to meditation—instead of detention. The result is that we have classrooms where children know how to concentrate and learn at a much faster pace than traditional schools."

The message was loud and clear. What A-Luv was learning wasn't just because he had hit a phase in his life where he had material success and needed to figure out what else there was to life. These teachings applied to everyone. And when a kid learns them, imagine the impact it would have on the rest of their life. He shook his head in amazement. *Why isn't this in every school?*

"The kids are actually out of class now and most have gone home, but we do have some kids who need to stay later, so we make it fun for them. They play games with volunteers who come in from around the community to give them love and joy."

They walked from the garden to a huge mango tree. Guddu plucked a mango and said, "When a tree bears lots of fruit, it has no choice but to bow down. Like the tree, we must help others when we have lots of success. The more success, the more we help. Sometimes the tree has lots of leaves and fruit and other times it is bare. But no matter what, the tree is still there. You may have wealth and it may go, but what can't be taken from you will always remain."

They continued to walk, entered a building, and passed a few classrooms till they reached a set of double doors. When it opened, they entered a stunning indoor gymnasium where kids danced to Bollywood music banging

from the speakers and subwoofers. And there in the front
of the class teaching the kids, was Nikki. She moved her
body so fluidly, with steps A-Luv had never seen before.
Her eyes were so expressive that they seemed part of the
dance too. Nikki's hips swayed, her feet stomped, and
her hands elegantly moved from one position to another.
Some of the kids followed her choreography while others
moved to their own beat. A-Luv's heart skipped a beat.

Nina waved at Nikki, who waved back, and then her eyes
met with A-Luv's. She flashed him a pearly white smile,
looked down in shyness and back up to meet his gaze.
When the song stopped, Nikki switched off the music and
gave the kids some instruction to practice on their own.
When she walked over, she pressed her palms together to
greet Nina, touched Guddu's feet, and gave A-Luv a huge
hug. "Did you enjoy your day on the river?"

"Yeah, glad to be alive in more ways than one! Can't wait
to tell you about it. So wait, you volunteer here too?"

"I do. Usually two or three times a week. As much as I
can, really."

"Nikki does a lot more than that too. This gymnasium was
built from her donations."

How on earth can she do so much? She runs the entire

yoga retreat center, practices meditation every day, does yoga, teaches classes, and now I find out she volunteers and donated enough money to build a gym. I am totally blown away. I already think she's pretty amazing but now I don't even have words. I can't wait to get back to the retreat center and tell her what happened today. She's gonna flip when she hears how I almost died. I mean, I think she'll flip. I don't really know how she'll react. I don't even care; I just want to tell her, simply to share with her. Whoa, you just want to share with her? Yeah, I do. You heard that, right? Yup.

"You never cease to surprise me, Nikki. What made you get involved here?"

"It felt natural, really. I have been so blessed in my life and I felt that these kids who come from low-income families deserved a shot at better educational opportunities. When Gudduji and Auntie were planning to build the school it called my heart, so I helped however I could. I initially thought to create a yoga hall to teach asanas and meditation, but as I began visualizing it through meditation, the vision evolved into something much bigger. Now we have this all-purpose gymnasium."

"You all make me feel so inspired. Thank you for sharing this with me and for all you're doing for these kids. I would love to get involved and see how we can spread this high vibe lifestyle to other schools and communities back in the US. Matter of fact, how dope would it be to teach kids music too! I can imagine instruments, beat making, writing rhymes..."

Nikki giggled. "I love your enthusiasm," she said. "You see how this is all within you. Take time and see what inspiration sticks. Sometimes ideas come our way and they are not for us to act on. Other ideas are perfectly suited for us. I wonder if ideas sometimes move from person to person until they've found the right home. That's why you see someone else doing an idea you've had before. Take your time and go through the steps in meditation. When you begin to visualize in HD, you will realize what you're meant to do. We have a few months ahead of us together, I'll help you."

And that's all A-Luv needed to hear. They bid the children farewell. When they arrived back at the main office, it was time for them to say goodbye to Nina as well. Guddu and Nina gave each other a big hug followed by another big laugh. A-Luv touched her feet once more and she gave him her blessings. "It was lovely to meet you, and please don't be a stranger. FaceTime me sometimes, let me know how you are doing. I will do the same. Keep learning and putting those lessons into practice. Guddu is an excellent guide for you and I can see he's found the right people to help you in your journey." She looked at Nikki from the corner of her eye. She gave A-Luv a big hug.

Nikki asked, "Do you want to ride with me?"

"Uh, yeah! Deuces, Guddu."

"Ah ah ah ah ah ah ah ah ah ah ah ah ah!!!" roared Guddu.

"Ha ha ha ha ha ha ha ha ha ha ha ha ha!!!" laughed A-Luv in unison.

SINGULAR

7

SINGULAR

The short car ride back to the retreat center was just enough time for A-Luv to tell Nikki about his near-death experience and its lessons. She admired his storytelling ability and found her awareness vacillating between what he was saying and how he was saying it. For his part, A-Luv enjoyed telling stories, especially to Nikki. She listened with an open heart, no judgment, and always kept her focus on him. A-Luv found that a few minutes with her was a heightened experience, each and every time.

They arrived at the center. Although A-Luv wanted to keep talking, Nikki graciously redirected him, mentioning that dinner was being prepared and she needed to check in on some things. Perhaps he would like to shower and then join her?

As A-Luv made his way to the dining area, there were

hundreds of people in the hall. Up until now, he had eaten only with Guddu and Nikki, so he was a little surprised at how many people were actually there. He spotted a table where Guddu and Nikki sat. To his delight, some of the musicians, editors, and writers from the studio joined them. He took a seat and was served a vegetarian *thali,* an Indian-style platter with a selection of various dishes served on a silver plate. The vibe in the dining area was welcoming and inclusive. A-Luv didn't know anyone yet, but he felt part of the community already. Guddu raised his glass of mango *lassi,* looked at A-Luv, and made a toast. "Now you know what to do. It is time for you to practice. To the newest yogi, cheers!"

LIFE'S A GAME.

LET'S PLAY!

Before meeting Guddu, A-Luv never would have imagined a transformation from suffering to joy was possible so quickly. He used to become quickly annoyed when things didn't go his way. When his ego wished for something to be a certain way and it didn't turn out, he would feel angst, anxiety, and pain. He didn't know that, all this time, he had within him the ability to feel joy despite those things happening. He had seen too many fellow artists suffer in their lives and die too soon from feuds, drug overdoses, suicides, obesity, stress, and other ailments.

He understood that his lost friendships, failed relationships, estranged family, drug dependence, and unhealthy habits were all energy drains that caused him to spiral downward and close his heart.

Now that his heart felt open, he would sooner die than let it close again. He had gained a new perspective on relationships that had gone bad and realized the resolution didn't need to happen between him and that person—in fact, it never would—but that the resolution needed to happen within. He couldn't rock all-white Cortez's in a heart and mind filled with dirt. He saw life for what it truly was, all one big game. Material success could come or not, but what mattered most was his ability to have fun and play.

Guddu showed him the ills of the distracted lifestyle and

the rush of being present, experiencing each second to its fullest. He never knew that the mind wasn't him, that he was actually the one in control of the mind. Guddu taught him that being without thought doesn't mean you're dumb, it means you have the ability to stay so present that you don't need the constant chatter. A-Luv saw that chatter like he saw music. He could picture a sheet of music with note after note stacked one after another, like the endless chatter of the mind creating thought after thought. That wouldn't be music; that would be a constant buzz of noise. He realized that the beauty in music came from the space between each note. Without the space, there is no harmony. The same applied to his thoughts. Without creating space between thoughts, he couldn't let in creativity. Sure, drugs and extreme sports could do the trick, but those were a crutch. All he really needed was to learn to stop thoughts through meditation and apply that to his waking life. All the creativity would pour in, and his curiosity was so intense that he made presence his main goal.

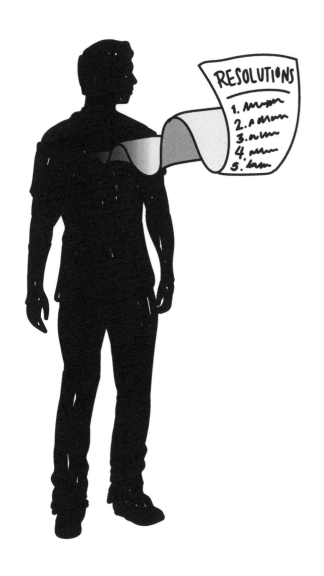

**ALL RESOLUTIONS
HAPPEN WITHIN**

The next few months were a whole new way of experiencing life for A-Luv. He woke up every morning without checking texts or emails and headed straight to the meditation hall to join Nikki's class. After class, he'd eat breakfast and would wander to different places to sit and write. He realized that he could induce flow state by keeping totally present, by using his willpower to concentrate, and channeling whatever came through him without judgment. He was already a singer-songwriter, but the songs came to him at a pace so intense, all he could do was hang on to the pen and write.

After lunch, he'd walk around the gardens, sit on rocks at the river's edge, or hike into the Himalayas to tune his ear to new sounds and record them. Then he'd head into the studio to learn the sounds of Indian instruments, play with nature's sounds, and allow inspiration to pour into him. He had never been a beatmaker, but that wasn't a story he told himself anymore. He wasn't trying to make a song that sounded like something else. He was making what felt like him.

At night after dinner, he would get together with Nikki—sometimes in the studio so she could hear what he was working on, and other times for an evening stroll. They shared stories about their past, their families and friends, and experiences that touched them. Sometimes they'd call it early and other times they'd talk late into the night, losing track of time. That made for a challenging meditation the next morning, so Nikki came up with an idea after a couple weeks and introduced A-Luv to yoga poses, or *asanas*. They would get up extra early before meditation. She showed him the various poses and helped him sink into each position to a point that felt right for him. This was totally different than the high-intensity workouts he was used to that required weights and rush. After a month of practicing yoga, eating on the floor, and sitting cross-legged while writing, he had built up the core strength to meditate on the floor, without needing a chair.

His writings continued to pour through him and new imagery, rhyme schemes, and stories emerged. He took on social issues as an advocate for the hip-hop community but was also willing to turn the lens on himself and sing about issues he perpetuated that plagued the hip-hop scene. He wasn't a stranger to materialism and consumerism. He realized the bling around your neck was simply a shiny golden noose that tightens the more you pursue it.

The real bling wasn't actually an object, it was the subject. As a poetic writer, he understood the subject-object agreement in a sentence structure applied to the self and everything else. Emotions, thoughts, actions, things, experiences, situations, personalities, and people are all objects. The subject is you. The soul. He had lost himself in the external where the subject became the object. Guddu showed him how to awaken his soul, to once again separate the subject from the object and never lose his true nature to those things again.

He explored Indian music in a wide range of forms, from the contemporary Bollywood and Bhangra to distinctly unique forms like Qawwali and Bhajans. He came to understand the Indian music that sounded so unknown and unrecognizable at first. It became the most natural thing. He began to combine Sufi imagery with soul, the samples picked up in nature and the sounds from Indian instruments, with the backbone and energy of hip-hop.

He took risks and was very frank about his music and about the choices he made. You could hear all his background and his journey in his music. He was willing to use elements in his music that were not popular, and he was willing to do things melodically that weren't popular, either. He played instruments that had been heard before, but not in this way. He allowed different worlds to collide and found the most beautiful angle in each, screenshotted it, and made that the bed of his songs. He fused together two styles and made a third. The fusion of east and west became a union. His flows communicated lyrics in a way that was natural to the beats but had never been done before. There was nothing to compare it to, because he was doing him. His music was singular.

CREATIVITY
POURS INTO THE

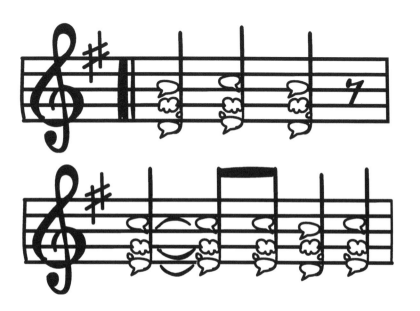

SPACE BETWEEN
THOUGHTS

With his heart open, music continued to pour into him, and so did the unexpected: love. He respected Nikki at so many levels: for her ability to run this operation, her yoga and meditation teachings, her giving heart as a volunteer and donor, and as an open-hearted person who vibed at the same level as him. And without having to discuss it, he could feel that her heart was open for him the same way. While he had been in relationships before, he was in India and this was an Indian girl, so he sought the advice of his guru.

He shared with Guddu that he was in love with Nikki but that he didn't know what that meant for an Indian girl. He assumed there was no dating but didn't understand how it worked. Guddu was thrilled and said he saw it from day one. "I could see it from the moment you met. I'm surprised it took you so long."

"Guddu, it's only been twenty-five days since I met her."

"Ah ah ah ah ah ah ah ah ah ah ah!!

"Well, you are right, you cannot apply your western template in India. You must accept that there is no dating here. Either you love her and want to marry her, or you don't. Then your parents will talk with her parents to make sure everyone gives their blessing. The blessings of your family are a gift for your relationship. I will speak with her parents first, since I am here and her parents are, too. Then we will introduce your parents to them. When all the blessings are received, you have an engagement ceremony and then a wedding. *Bas,* simple."

That would have been overwhelming for A-Luv to take in before. He had many relationships in the past but had never married. Something always blocked him. He realized he had closed his heart and never truly accepted the person he was with, because he had never truly accepted who he was himself. Now, with his heart fully open and unwilling to let it close, he accepted the situation, understood the choices, and decided he would ask her to marry him. And even though Guddu told him there was an engagement ceremony where the engagement ring was placed on the girl's hand, A-Luv had always imagined himself getting on one knee to propose. Only thing was, he needed a ring. Fortunately, he knew a guy.

Within a day, Guddu and A-Luv designed an engagement ring and sent the designs to Guddu's ringmaker in Jaipur, a city renowned for its jewelry. On the 28th day from the day they met, A-Luv arranged to have dinner with Nikki while his musician friends played Qawwali music in the background. At the end of dinner, the waiter brought out a rose and handed it to A-Luv. A-Luv got down on one knee, without a ring, and asked for Nikki's hand in marriage. She said yes with tears of joy in her eyes.

Nikki went to share the news with her parents that night and A-Luv told his parents. The joy from both sides was overwhelming. A-Luv told Guddu who, as promised, first spoke with Nikki's parents and then arranged the conversation between both sets of parents. All gave their blessing, and A-Luv went to meet Nikki's family. They accepted him wholeheartedly and would meet A-Luv's parents soon for the engagement.

Guddu had already begun making arrangements for an engagement party unlike any other. His ringmaker traveled by train overnight to deliver the ring in person. Guddu and A-Luv went down to Gangama and dipped the ring in the holy water to ask Mother Earth for her blessing. The engagement party was set on Ganga Kinare, or the banks of the Ganges River, with hundreds of people to attend. It would be perfect.

As the day of the engagement approached, hundreds of family members from the US and India arrived to celebrate and offer their blessings. The media never caught a whisper of the engagement, so there was no paparazzi or unnecessary attention to distract from the ceremony.

A-Luv had something special planned. His musician friends formed a band. Together, they would perform a few songs A-Luv had written and composed in honor of his bride-to-be.

The night of the engagement was the first time A-Luv's and Nikki's parents met. Though they were shy at first, they quickly grew comfortable with each other. After all, A-Luv's family was also Indian. To everyone's pleasant surprise, both families were from the same state in India, which meant they shared the same language, food, customs, and music.

Guddu got onto the stage, welcomed everyone, and thanked them for coming. He made sure everyone had plenty to eat and asked that they come take their seat on the huge lawn overlooking the river, as the ceremony was about to begin. "First, there is a surprise for you. Ladies and gentlemen, please welcome to the stage, A-Luv and the Omboys!"

The stage curtain opened. There, in the center of the stage, was A-Luv with his signature gold microphone and a custom flatbill hat with a logo no one had ever seen before: a hip-hop stylized ōm symbol.

On stage was a drummer, tabla player, bass guitarist, sitar player, keyboardist, a DJ—and A-Luv. The drummer tapped four times and the beat kicked in. A-Luv grabbed his gold mic and flowed straight from his soul out to the gathered families. When the last song finished, Nikki rushed up to the stage and gave A-Luv a huge hug. She was filled with love and adored seeing her man perform.

Their engagement ceremony began shortly thereafter. A-Luv finally placed the engagement ring on Nikki's finger. Everyone celebrated the night away, already looking forward to attending the five-day wedding in three months.

During that time, A-Luv planned to return with his family back to LA and bring his high vibe lifestyle with him. The couple didn't want to be apart for a minute, but they accepted the situation and were well equipped to handle the separation.

Saying goodbye to Guddu wasn't going to be easy. Guddu changed his life, and the two of them had grown quite fond of each other. Although they would keep in touch and visit one another, they would miss each other. Guddu brought A-Luv into his shop before he left for the airport. He brought out a beaded mala.

"This is for you," he said. "It is a *rudraksha* mala and has very special energy which will help you. There are 108 beads plus one on this mala. 108 is a sacred number and the one bead has a symbolic value as the *guru* bead. These seeds come from a very specific type of tree which you will find here in India and many countries throughout the world. The original tree is in Indonesia, and these seeds are all Indonesian which means they are very rare. Each bead has between one and twenty-one *mukhi,* or sides. Almost all *rudraksha* you will find are four, five, and six *mukhis* as that is most common. The rarest in the world is known as *ek mukhi,* or one side.

"Maharaji told me that the only thing I should never sell in my shop is an *ek mukhi,* so I never do. He said it so rare that it is the closest thing to the energy source, so you cannot put a price on it. I never sell *ek mukhi,* I only give it away.

"On your mala, I have put an *ek mukhi* there. You also have a five *mukhi* representing the five elements from which your body is made, seven *mukhi* which represents Maha Laxmi, eight *mukhi* for Ganesha, eleven *mukhi* representing all *rudras,* twelve *mukhi* for the sun, and for the guru bead, a double-joint *mukhi* with twelve faces representing Shiva, Shakti, and the sun. Just on the top of it, I've added a gold tassel. This is not something for your ego. This is something for you. When you see someone with a tassel standing out from their shirt behind their neck, you will know they are wearing a mala inside and what that means. Be sure that no one holds your mala, because their energy will transfer to it and then to you. Do not let it touch the ground, and wear it under your shirt so it touches your skin directly. This will bring the strength of all that energy directly to you. It has been dipped in Gangama to bring you all the blessings from Mother Nature."

And with that, Guddu handed over the *rudraksha* mala. A-Luv placed it over his head and tucked it into his shirt. This was exactly how they sat when they first met. Guddu behind the glass display case and A-Luv in front of it. They stood up and Guddu moved from around the back of the display case to walk A-Luv out. They reached the front of the showroom, and A-Luv bent down to touch Guddu's feet. Guddu touched the top of A-Luv's head and blessed him, *kush raho*. They hugged tightly and Guddu said, "I love you."

"I love you too, Guddu."

BLING IS ADORNED IN YOUR SOUL

During A-Luv's performance at the engagement, hundreds of live videos went up on social media, and within seconds, the performance went viral. People couldn't believe this was A-Luv. It looked like him, but it didn't sound like him. And it certainly didn't sound like anything anyone had ever heard before. The media followed him everywhere now that he was back in the States. In the past, this would drive him crazy with anger. Now, he simply accepted that this was part of his life and he chose to stay present without giving the media his energy. He had all the privacy he needed inside himself and no one could take that from him.

A-Luv continued his daily high vibe practice and spent most of his time in the studio, writing lyrics, assembling beats, layering in Indian sounds, dropping verses, and mixing and mastering all the songs he created in Laxman Jhula. He had created seven songs while he was there and he decided to publish the album. The album's cover contained what would become an iconic image: his signature ōm. The symbol became a viral sensation as it symbolized the union of hip-hop and yogic cultures.

The album immediately topped the charts when it dropped, but that didn't matter to A-Luv or Nikki. What happened was much bigger than they could have ever predicted. After getting married in India and moving to the US, the culture of hip-hop began to shift, and its far-reaching influence carried throughout the world. With fans streaming his music worldwide, A-Luv brought the high vibe lifestyle into the lives of millions around the world and its influence on hip-hop helped shift the culture from material to spiritual.

Bling was no longer something adorned on the body—it was something adored in the soul.

THE END

NEXT STEPS IN YOUR JOURNEY

Congratulations and thank you for investing your energy to read this story. I hope you've learned a lot and are ready to begin your own transformational journey. So where do you go from here? Now that you've learned all these lessons, how can you engrain them into your mind so that they're easy to recall whenever you need to put them into practice?

Here are four (free) things you can do to begin your journey:

Download the *Bling* album. I produced a hip-hop album—the first of its kind—as a soundtrack to the book. Each chapter in the book inspired each track. Seven chapters, seven tracks, and each track is fire. Every book comes with a free album download. Get yours here: www.andyseth.com/blingthealbum

Download the *illest*rations. There are 52 custom illustrations—or *illest*rations as I call them—in the book. One for every week in the year or enough to fill a deck of cards. Download a set of these illustrations to use as wallpapers here: www.andyseth.com/blingillustrations

Listen to my guided meditation. I'll guide you through the same meditation that Nikki taught A-Luv so that you can practice this technique on a daily basis. Download the guided meditation here: www.andyseth.com/blingmeditation

Join our private Facebook group. I'll respond to questions here so that you have direct access to answers as you go on your journey. I'll also share helpful tips, exclusive content, and invite guests to share their lessons with you. Join "The High Vibe Tribe" here: https://www.facebook.com/groups/andysethtribe

Consider these resources as just the start of your journey and be sure to help your friends and family thrive by sharing this book with them as well. Follow the high vibe lifestyle and watch life unfold beyond your imagination.

ACKNOWLEDGMENTS

Among the many blessings I count, this book wouldn't have happened without the unconditional love and support from my wife, Natasha Seth. You are not only the inspiration behind Nikki, you are the love of my life and I'm grateful you said yes in twenty-eight days.

To my mom, Anju Seth, who is the inspiration behind Nina. You have always blessed me with boundless love, showered me with praise, and shown me how joy and happiness can always be chosen, no matter how difficult the situation.

To my dad, Shiv Seth, for instilling in me a deep appreciation for music and the written word. Your love of Qawwali, Ghazals, poetry, and being the first person to translate the complete works of Manto, has shown me it's possible to bring music and writing together.

To my sister, Puja Seth, for being my guide through the yoga culture. You helped me understand how the high vibe lifestyle is practiced in the west vs. east, and the delicate balance that exists between the material and spiritual.

To Anil Idiculla, my soul brother and inspiration for AI in this book. Your love and generosity are unparalleled. This book wouldn't have happened without you providing me the space and comforts of your mountain home, allowing me to write in flow state.

To my editor, Demeris Morse. You are a shining example of someone living the high vibe lifestyle while creating inspirational work. Thank you for supporting me through the process to make sure my message is clear.

To Ashley Getty, my illustrator who helped me translate the story into one-of-a-kind visuals. You looked for the message behind each quote and poured creativity into each concept. Thank you for seeing my vision so clearly and turning words into art.

And finally, to Guddu *Mama*, my uncle. I know if I thank you, you'll tell me that you are simply the messenger. I'm going to thank you anyway. By anyone's standards, your level of material success is far beyond what anyone would imagine. But anyone who meets you knows that if all went away tomorrow, you would still have the same love in your heart. Thank you for teaching me that I can have joy and be at peace while playing the game of life to its fullest. Thank you for showing me everything is possible by the grace of God, and for teaching me the high vibe lifestyle.

ABOUT THE AUTHOR

ANDY SETH is a serial entrepreneur, author, and music producer who has founded nine successful businesses, helped thousands of individuals break the cycle of poverty, and raised millions through his charitable endeavors. He serves as the trustees chairman for Minds Matter, is a Governor's Fellow, and is a master diver.

Andy has been featured by national media outlets including CNBC, CBS, *The Huffington Post*, *Wall Street & Technology*, and Comcast Newsmakers. He has also won numerous awards including "Forty Under 40" and "Top 25 Most Influential in Colorado."

But things weren't always so cush. Until the age of fourteen, Andy lived in a Los Angeles motel with his sister and parents. He was an entrepreneur from the jump, launching his first business at the age of thirteen while earning full-ride scholarships to Culver Military Academy and Boston College.

He's a husband and father, and on any given day you'll find him meditating, volunteering, and running the nation's first digital agency founded with an apprenticeship program, Flow.

To book Andy to speak at your next event or to get down with more of his teachings, visit andyseth.com today.

Made in the USA
Monee, IL
07 November 2022